Can I Know God?

and other sermons

W. E. SANGSTER

Abingdon Press

New York   *Nashville*

CAN I KNOW GOD?

Published in Great Britain as
WESTMINSTER SERMONS—AT MORNING WORSHIP

Copyright © 1960 by Abingdon Press

Library of Congress Catalog Card Number: 61-5198

LITHO IN U. S. A.

For

MARY

with love

Preface

I AM A TRAVELING PREACHER UNABLE, BY REASON OF SICKNESS, either to travel or preach. A number of people have written to me suggesting that I publish a book of sermons.

I have resisted the idea in my mind for many months. I thought that they were being kind and were just seeking an occupation for a sick man. In my view a sermon is a peculiarly personal thing, fashioned by much thought and prayer in a preacher's mind, but normally made for a particular congregation at a particular time and largely fulfilling itself in its utterance. I said once to my own congregation at the Westminster Central Hall, "My sermons are not to be remembered, but translated." Grateful as I have been for half a dozen volumes of sermons I have met in my life, I have seen no reason for many years to add to their number and felt that the books I had published on the craft of homiletics were my maximum usefulness to young men practicing the preacher's calling.

That I finally decided to take the task in hand is due more to a book reviewer than to anybody else. Commenting in an article on several books on preaching (one of my own among them), he put in a plea "for books of sermons rather than books *about* sermons." He expressed the view that Tillotson's enormous influence (for good or ill) on the English pulpit did not derive from a book on homiletics but from the wide study of his sermons themselves. "Few of us want to preach other people's sermons," he said, "but many of us would like to see what other people say and how they put it." I was convinced by that. I suspect that my heart was aching all the time to continue the work I was ordained to do, but I felt sure now of the usefulness of the occupation, and I went to work.

But what sermons should I publish?

I must have preached thousands of sermons in nearly forty years of ministry. I have notes of many of them. How could I decide what would be most useful in print?

I settled the question this way. People who wrote urging that a book of sermons would be welcome, often said, "I remember your preaching on . . ." I was surprised how long ago some of the occasions were. Whether or not the sermons had been translated into life, I don't know, but they had been remembered. Perhaps, after all, that was a commendation! The sermon mentioned sometimes surprised me. I could hardly expect them, I suppose, to ask for one sustained expositional series—for any one would have taken the whole book. What I have taught on the work of Christ, the Cross, divine guidance, sanctity, evangelism, and simple apologetics they could read in my other writings. What makes a sermon gratefully memorable, I imagine, is its authoritative meeting of some deep personal need—and this is the fruit of God's response to the preacher's prayer for the right theme for the occasion.

I think I could have taken a handful of sermons more doctrinally deep and homiletically satisfying than these, but the test of a sermon, at the last, is not the evidence it gives of skilled craftsmanship, but whether it does the work. Whether or not it is evident, these sermons seem to have done the work, and the reader will be as ready as I am to ascribe their influence to the grace of God rather than to any ability of the preacher.

In the nature of things a printed sermon is a poor substitute for the preached word. There is a divine "mystique" in worship —in the setting of which our preaching is done—which cannot permeate a printing press. The majority of preachers—and I belong to their number—neither read nor recite their sermons. They go steeped in prayer and with their thoughts shaped and marshaled, their illustrations ready, a clear conviction how they will begin and end—but the actual phrasing they command in the moment of its utterance. They know by long and ineffable experience that there is a "plus of the Spirit" which no human skill can command—something God adds in the hour itself, which is born of his blessing on the prayers of people and preacher alike. It measures, I suppose, the length of a pause. It adds its own overtones and nuances. It leads you to say some things, at least, you had not intended, to linger here and speed there. There are, indeed, times when the Holy Spirit seems to "take over," and the preacher has that sublime experience of being just "spoken through."

How can *that* go into print? It just can't. All that I can do from the notes which survive is to set down the theme, give the substance of what was said, and hope that the condescending grace of God, which owned the word in its utterance, may be able to make some use of it when it is read.

It remains for me only to say a brief word about style and homiletical form, and then to indicate the kind of congregation I normally addressed.

A sermon is not an essay. If the sermonic note offends in an essay and is felt to be out of place (as, I think, it is), an essay is out of place in the pulpit. A sermon can combine exposition, rebuke, challenge, comfort . . . it calls for *direct speech*. A preacher can say "You." Indeed, he ought to say "You!" He can almost point—if he points to himself as well! Colloquialisms, which would normally appear as blemishes in an essay, have not to be rigidly excluded from the sermon. The preacher can lean out of his pulpit and, in an easy commerce with the pew, press home his point with "homely" words. The Saviour is his example in this as in everything else.

Normally, a sermon aims to do one thing, and it ought, therefore, to be a thing worth doing. Men sometimes waste their twenty to thirty minutes of sermon time on some marginal matter quite unworthy of the setting of worship or heap together unrelated trifles which leave no clear impression on the mind when, at last, they mercifully peter out. Except in a certain important category of strictly expositional sermons, and, perhaps, in Bible biographies too, one important thing should be the preacher's aim and, inevitably, it involves repetition. The people are not going to read the sermon—with the opportunity of glancing back and checking what was written—they are hearing it and hearing it once. If it is to be nailed home in their thought, it will take more than one tack to do it. The sermon becomes, therefore, the craft of skillful repetition; nail after nail; of saying the important thing again and again, but with such variety of phrasing and illustration that the repetition, so far from boring the congregation, sustains their interest to the last word and sends them away with the important truth hammered firmly on to the walls of their minds. All who listen will get good; some will get much good; and, for a few, it might be one of the great hours of their life. Rich reward, indeed, for all the prayer and preparation which went into shaping the sermon!

"Shaping" the sermon? Yes! A sermon, I am sure, must have "shape." Even untutored minds appreciate form and progression in an exposition or argument. They may not understand why, but they know when a sermon is "without form and, therefore, void." They know, also, when it begins crisply, takes shape, and moves up to the climax which they sense to be sound. It satisfies their minds (as well, one hopes, as reaching their hearts), and no preacher can succeed who has not respect for the minds of his hearers, however unacademic they may be. I hope those who read my pages will find "shape" in the sermons and bear in mind that repetition and swift recapitulations are all necessary parts of this form of the spoken word.

The congregations I normally addressed were composed, for the most part, of working-class and lower middle-class people. (Forgive the absurd terms!) I had my share of students and professional people, but for the most part, they were as I describe them. These people are, in any case, by far the larger part of the total community—and I liked it that way. People of this type are not helped by a parade of learning, or by too much academic language. They can understand the hardest things a preacher has to say if he will put it with reasonable simplicity and illustrate it well. They sit without intellectual pride, and their faces light up as your points register on their minds. To serve such people —and God through them—is a privilege of which no man is worthy. They chose, in their letters, the sermons I have published here.

My warmest thanks are due to Greville P. Lewis, B.A., B.D., for reading and commenting on what I have written, and to Miss Margaret Gregory for typing the manuscript.

W. E. SANGSTER

Contents

1

Can I Know God?

I know him whom I have believed—II Tim. 1:12

THE MOST DARING THING THE DEVOUT MAN EVER SAYS ABOUT HIS religion is "I know." Not "I think," "I hope," "I trust," "I venture," "I believe," but *"I know."*

He claims to know God for himself. He says (in effect) that in something of the same way by which a music lover enters into a new realm by lovely sound and the art lover enters into a new world by lovely color, so, by faith, he enters a realm where he transcends the faith he first needed, and now he can say *"I know."*

It is, of course, an extraordinary thing to say. To know God. To glimpse the purpose of existence. To be certain that in prayer, in worship, in the Bible, at the holy table, one truly has fellowship with the Ruler of the universe. The claim is quite staggering. Yet multitudes of rational people make it and are so sure of God that, when calamity overtakes them, they are still unshaken and confidently assert that—

> . . . One above
> In perfect wisdom, perfect love
> Is working for the best.

15

Put into precise terms, the experience which is claimed is one of immediate acquaintance. It is not "knowledge about," as I might have knowledge about, say, Bouvet Island in the South Atlantic (where I have never been and am never likely to go) but immediate acquaintance such as I had for years with my father, at whose side I grew up, on whose strength I relied, and to whom I could turn for help every day. The heart of religion is not an opinion about God, but a personal relationship *with* him. Judge yourself how near you are to the heart of religion by that!

Now I want to speak to you about the reliability of this awareness of God. Those of you—and they are many—who know all about this from the inside are not my chief concern now. (You may think of something else if you like.) I want to help people who are *seeking* this experience but haven't found it or who think they might be at the beginning of it but fear to be guilty of self-deception. Let me see if I can say something for the encouragement and conviction of these, and let me approach the theme in a similar way to Elton Trueblood in his Swarthmore Lecture, which I warmly commend.

Is God there? Can he be known by any man? Is the very claim to have direct contact with God vain, foolish, mistaken, and plainly a piece of self-deception? Or is it, as millions have claimed through the centuries, gloriously true, so that any man without it is like some poor, blind fellow stumbling through life, having never opened his eyes to the wonder and rapture of a world of light?

That is our task, and to that task I want to turn now.

I

Now, how can you test at any time what we call the "objectivity" or reality of an experience? How can you prove, that is to say, that you are not deceiving yourself, that there *is* something outside which corresponds to your experience?

Suppose a man were suffering from d.t.'s. Not many of you will know that sickness from experience (!), but if you have ever witnessed it—and a minister of religion sees most diseases after years of visitation—you know that a man so suffering is sure that he can *see* things, queer, strangely shaped animals coming over the end of the bed and making for him.

Or, if I may borrow an illustration from the desert, any man who has traveled across the desert knows the deceptions of the mirage. I have seen the mirage many times in the desert of Sinai. You see the water in front of you. You would take your oath that it is there—and, just as you reach it, it fades away.

These human senses of ours are subject to illusions like that, and the great fear which gnaws at the heart of many honest people in regard to religious impression is that this talk of fellowship with God is some superior form of self-delusion. How do we test, therefore, what we call the "objectivity" of an experience (i.e. the fact that it is real) in any walk of life?

Well, we normally subject it to three tests.

First, we ask whether the testimony of one sense is confirmed by the others. A man suffering from d.t.'s can never touch the animals he thinks he sees, or a man in the desert, deceived by the mirage, can never drink the water he believes is there. We test the testimony of one sense by the others.

In the second place, if we are dependent for our belief that something has happened on the report of witnesses, we inquire how many people had the experience and how dependable they are as reporters.

Finally, we inquire whether this experience fits into our knowledge of the world as a whole and whether it is confirmed by other sources of knowledge concerning total reality.

17

Can we apply those tests to this question of the reliability of religious experience?

You cannot apply the first test because religious experience is not a stimulant of sense; it doesn't come to us by taste, touch, hearing, sight, or smell. It is not "material."

As to the third test, you can apply it, but I am not proposing to work on that aspect of the subject now.

I believe that the existence of God can be established as an enormous probability apart from its basis in religious experience, but I am convinced that I shall help you most, and come nearest to succeeding in my task, if I concentrate now on the second test.

(1) Are the people who claim to have fellowship with God sufficiently numerous for us to believe that all human beings might share it? (2) Are the witnesses not only numerous but are they dependable? Can they be completely trusted? (3) Are the reports which they bring mutually consistent, so that even though their testimony be divided by hundreds of years in time and their place of residence half a world apart, we can feel, when they speak about their knowledge of God, that they are speaking about the same thing?

Let us look at those three tests in turn.

II

1. I say the reporters must be sufficiently numerous.

Things can be true and yet so rare as almost to be freakish and to have no special significance for the race as a whole. For instance every century or so "a calculating boy" is born, a child with the ability to multiply, divide, add, subtract, and do all sorts of amazingly clever things with figures absolutely at sight. Zerah Colburn, who was born in America but was in Britain as a lad of seven in 1812, would be a case in point. He was the calculating boy *par excellence*. It seemed that no numbers were too big for him. He was asked on examination by British experts (among other more erudite questions) how many minutes there were in forty-eight years, and he flashed the answer back instantly. Before they could write it down he told them, for good measure, how many *seconds* there were in forty-eight years as well!

He was seven years old.

It was true—but it was freakish. It tells you nothing about the capacities of ordinary people.

But the religious experience I am speaking of is not like that. It is not the experience of the few rare people who hear audible voices and see visions. I believe that there are such people, but they are not the basis of my reasoning now. I contend that there are millions of plain folk who have an awareness of the sustaining love of God and enjoy the presence of the Divine Companion without audible voices and describable visions. They would say in all honesty, "I know him whom I have believed."

If we were to consider only the testimony of the "evangelicals," how many myriads throughout the world have passed through their "experience" meetings and borne witness to their personal intimacy with God?

We can say quite positively, then, as we come to examine the testimony to this experience, that there are *millions* of reporters.

2. In the second place, if we are to believe in the reality of an experience like this, the reporters must be *dependable* witnesses. We must be sure both of the judgment and character of the people who speak in this way.

Now, it is certain that this religious witness is not the testimony of people lying in the interests of trade. Some advertisers will say anything to sell their goods, but this is not a vast conspiracy of people who keep saying a thing, not because it is true, but because they want to make money out of it. These are the finest souls our race has produced. This is the testimony of people of character. This is the witness of the saints, some famous, but infinitely more of them obscure.

Think of the glorious company of the apostles. Think of the goodly fellowship of the prophets. Think of the noble army of martyrs. Think of the Holy Church throughout all the world. It is, indeed, a vast concourse of people marching through the centuries and crying in confident chorus: "We know that he abideth in us."

The man who sets out to prove that this experience is an illusion has taken on a harder task than he knows. To suggest that anybody who makes this claim is at least a little mad is to challenge man's whole ability to appreciate values. If these, the great and glorious ones of the universe, are mad, who is balanced? If these are deranged, then derangement is more beautiful, more reasonable, more beneficent, more effective than sanity.

Oh, yes, the witnesses are not only numerous; they are truly worthy as well.

3. And notice, finally, that the reporters are consistent with one another. It has sometimes been said, though quite falsely, that it is difficult to correlate what the saints say about God and the spiritual world, because they all bear a different witness.

They do *not* bear a different witness.

I could put before you now the testimony of men and women who lived hundreds of years apart from one another, came from different races, and grew up in different ecclesiastical communions, but, as you read their testimony, you would see the essential coherence of it all: Blaise Pascal, the Roman Catholic; Isaac Pennington, the Quaker; John Fletcher, the Methodist; John Bunyan, the Independent; Charles Spurgeon, the Baptist; John Keble, the High Churchman; Handley Moule, the Low

Churchman—all their testimonies harmonize. They are speaking of the same experience. They know!

What a weight of testimony! Can you resist it? Are you, my friends, to whom I am especially addressing myself, content to sit there and be reminded of the weight and the quality and the coherence of this witness, and brush it all aside and say, "There is nothing in it; *I* have never had such an experience? Are you the final test of truth? You are too modest to think so! Things can be true though, so far, they have not come within your own experience.

Face this fact; it is possible to *know* God; it is possible for mortals in this shadowed world to have fellowship with the All Highest. If you shut yourself out from that experience, you are (as I say) like some poor, blind fellow stumbling through life with his eyes closed to the wonder and rapture of the world of light.

III

Yet I am aware that, despite this massive testimony, doubts will still linger in the mind of some of you to whom this faith borders on the incredible; and because I want you to believe, I would not close without another effort to convince your mind.

Those of us who have often talked these things over with friends who find faith hard have noticed that there are two obdurate objections which remain when others have been destroyed, and to one or the other of which I have known men to cling in the very last ditch of their fight against the Christian religion.

Let me see if I can deal briefly with each of them in turn.

1. It is urged by some objectors that if God were there, he would be more obvious, that everybody would be aware of him. Often these objectors crave for some material proof, like the medical student who complained to me at a religious "Brains

Trust" in a London hospital that he had dissected many bodies but found no trace of a soul.

Well, as we said before, God is not a stimulation of sense. We learn of material things by our material senses, but values—and God himself—come to us a different way. If we want to study the stars, we need good sight and a good telescope. The star is a material object and comes to us by material means.

But God is not a "thing." The preparation for seeing God is of a different kind. We need silence—a great deal of silence, a conscience quiet and unaccusing, faith enough to wait until he moves to us, a willingness to be taught by those whose quality of living gives support to their claim to know, an intelligent study of the Book which has fed the souls of millions, a most especial attention to the person and appeal of Christ himself.

All this takes time, of course, but could time be put to *better* use?

The testimony of the vast majority of those who have persisted in fulfilling these conditions is that they became aware of the "Presence," and the more they found, the way they sought. Some, it is true, have not found God, but they are few, I think, among earnest seekers and may be compared, I suppose, to the physically blind whom, we trust, will see clearly in eternity. But far the most of those who fulfill God's conditions meet the God they are passionately seeking in their hearts. The Great Other is there. Mortal man can be aware of him.

That, I think, is the answer to the first objection. Different aspects of reality can only be known in their own way: physical things by sense perception, values—and God—by contemplation. Do you sincerely feel that you have persistently sought God in the way he can be found?

2. Secondly, some people dismiss all this talk of religious experience on the ground that it is just "wishful thinking." Some-

times they argue that man has invented God because he is afraid of death and the dark, and sometimes they argue that in the same way as children have imaginary playmates so God is the "imaginary playmate" of the adult.

We know, of course, that children *do* have imaginary playmates, especially "only" children.

You that are parents know all about that. The only little child invents a playmate of his or her own age, gives him a name, is constantly talking about him—but he has no reality except in the child's imagination.

Our critics say that it is like that with religious people and God.

The whole answer to that objection would be perhaps a trifle long, but it is a very complete one, believe me.

Time allows me only to indicate to you one reason why this suggested "proof" of how man invented God is unconvincing.

The imaginary playmate is always a person whose wishes and desires harmonize with the mind of the one who invents him.

You notice that with little children. The imaginary playmate is always agreeable, always at hand, ready to change the game according to the desires of his human friend, and if he is a little stubborn now and then, he soon comes around.

This is what our critics ask us to believe: that religious people have invented a fiction-God who will always play the game our way.

But that isn't our God! Our God's demands are often at complete variance with our wishes. He says to many of our desires, "Thou shalt not." He holds back the swelling tide of human passion and, again and again, demands immense sacrifice from us.

The very psychology on which these critics rely is all against them when it comes to close examination.

Why not give this quest for the awareness of the Divine an unhurried trial? Is there, in all this universe, anything more important to you than to know God? Can you expect to know him in scamped moments? Are you willing to meet his conditions when he says, "Ye shall seek me and find me when ye shall search for me with all your heart"?

Give time to it, plenty of time. Go into the silence for long periods but also into the company of those who claim to know him. Put yourself to school to the Bible. Be found regularly at worship. Hold in your mind the picture of God revealed by Jesus and just think and think on him.

Don't lose heart if the hours go by and nothing seems to come. The hours are not being wasted. Persist! Faith will grow in you. The glad day will come when you also will say, "I know him whom I have believed."

2

Remember to Forget!

God . . . hath made me forget.—Gen. 41:51

WE OFTEN READ ADVERTISEMENTS IN THE NEWSPAPERS FOR systems of mind and memory training. We regard it as a great natural endowment if anybody has the gift for recalling a face, a fact, a name, just when he wants it. We say, "He has a good memory," and we feel that he is a man to be envied.

Nevertheless, I want to convince you that precious though a good memory is the power to *forget* is hardly less precious as well. If I were a teacher of mental efficiency, and giving all my time to the training of minds, I should make it my close concern not only to teach people how to remember, but to teach them also how to forget. Henri Bergson, the French philosopher said, "It is the function of the brain to enable us not to remember but to forget."

Some of you smile and say you have that gift already; you don't want any training in that. "I can *forget* all right," you say. "I can forget my wife's birthday. I can forget the day we were married. I can forget the present I promised to buy her. I don't want any training in forgetfulness. I am an expert already."

I wonder if you are the expert that you think? If you are forgetting your wife's birthday, you are forgetting a date you ought

25

to remember, but, at the same time, you may be remembering something you ought to forget.

Distinguished men are often forgetful in the sense of being what we call "absent-minded," and there is no denying that it causes a great deal of inconvenience. Temple Gairdner, the great missionary to Egypt, was a sinner in this way. It was most noticeable in the days when he was a secretary for the Christian Union. His colleague, Tissington Tatlow, says:

Every garment he possessed came back to the office through the post. Shoes, Bible, sponge, pajamas, toothbrush, waistcoat, and I know not what, followed one another in an unending stream to the delight of our office boy. On one occasion, he met a man in New Street, Birmingham, and put down his bag to make a note in his diary. When the note was made he went on blithely down New Street, minus the bag.

There is no denying that such kinds of forgetfulness cause other people inconvenience. Nobody ought lightly to indulge themselves in such a weakness. A man who often forgets an appointment; a man who is constantly neglectful of detail; a woman who fails her friends after promising and then says, with a little giggle, "Oh, I forgot," all these need to be taught pretty sternly how to remember. But if I were asked what caused more trouble in the world, the things forgotten that should have been remembered or the things remembered that should have been forgot, I'm sure I should fix on the latter. A bad memory has caused much trouble, but a bad forgettery, I fancy, has caused even more.

Let me see if I can convince you, first, of the importance of forgetting; secondly, indicate the things which ought to be forgotten; and, thirdly, show you how you may firmly acquire the art.

I

Think for a moment of the blessings of forgetfulness when it is just a natural consequence of the passage of time and not the outcome of conscious effort. When Joseph became a man of substance in Egypt and began to enjoy the quiet peace of married life, a son was born to him whom he named Manasseh. And the meaning of that name is this: "God has made me forget."

He looked back over his past—flung into a pit, sold by his own brothers, slandered by a lascivious woman, thrust into prison. . . . But now it was all behind him and the bitterness was passing out of his soul. "God has made me forget," he said.

Does God make us forget? Is it a boon that the sharp edge comes off our memory with the passing of time?

I think it is. Do you remember, even faintly, the floodtide of feeling when you were first bereaved? Was it sudden?—and stunning in its suddenness? Or did you have time to get ready for it but found, at the last, that you hadn't got ready at all? Can you recall your feelings at the time? The sun went out; the world was grey; purpose died in your heart; there was nothing, nothing, nothing to live for. When you saw the coffin, you wished you were in it yourself. You only longed to die. Can you remember?

Now, thank God, the edge has come off that first terrible sense of grief. You have not forgotten. Oh no! you have not, and you cannot fully forget, but the bewildering shock of it and the cutting acuteness of it have passed. Time hasn't healed, but time has helped.

In *that* degree God has made you forget. Thank him for it. Life would have been unliveable but for that beneficent dealing with you. Mercy has taken the edge from your sorrow. The scar is there still—a great rent across your heart—but it isn't an open wound, and there is no gangrene in it. God . . . God has made you forget.

Now, that is just an illustration of what I might call natural forgetfulness, the balm of time applied to a raw wound. Never forget that conscious memory has a preference for the pleasant. She is always trying to stuff painful experiences down the hole of oblivion and to preserve only the things we are glad to recall. The deeper laws of the mind are working with your will to help you to forget. Most of the things you want to forget want to be forgotten; you are not working *against* but *with* nature if you learn to forget. Yet natural memory alone cannot deal with all unpleasant things. It starts us right (for nature is God's servant), but we must find ways of working with it.

That is why I want to discuss the *art* of forgetting. My plea is this: that we may work together with God for the erasure of certain things from our minds, or, at least, their partial erasure— things that he wants us to forget and the mental storage of which is highly perilous.

Some psychologists believe that it is impossible to forget anything, that all our thoughts and deeds are stored up inside us, and that, though they may be beyond the reach of recollection, they are not really outside our present mental make-up. You see their point? You may not be able to *recall* them at will, but they are not forgotten.

That is an academic point which I cannot pause now to discuss. I believe that God will help us to forget things, the memory of which would do us harm, or rather that he will enable us to remember only so much of them as will be for our good and we, ourselves, not emotionally overwhelmed.

As I write, I can see on the top of my finger a scar; it is faint and barely perceptible, but it is there. I remember how it came. I nearly chopped the top of that finger off when I was a child. I have some dim recollection of the hospital and a few stitches, but it is very dim. I've forgotten the pain, and my finger is not misshapen or unsightly. The scar is faintly there, but I hardly notice it from one year's end to another. It is all but forgotten.

There are things in our past that can be as dim as that. The pain endured. The lesson learned. Let it now be forgotten! Face the future with courage, cheerfulness, and hope. Give God the chance, and he will make you forget all that it would be harmful to remember.

In most of the experiences of our past there is something to remember and something to forget.

Let us suppose that a man has failed in business. He was no scoundrel, but, in certain things, he was not prudent, and his failure has involved others in loss. If he just broods and broods on his failures, it will disable him; he may grow bitter, may even become insane.

Yet, if he can step past that sense of awful humiliation and just garner from his experience the practical wisdom it had to teach, he might start again, win through, perhaps, to substantial success, and repay his creditors as well.

There is something to remember, something to forget.

Let me talk now of the things I want you to forget.

II

1. Beginning with the less important things first, I want you to forget your gaucheries or, to put it in plain English, your tactlessnesses or to put it still plainer, "the bricks you've dropped."

I have been amazed at the number of people who have overcome the great sorrows of their life but who cannot recall the silly things they said on certain occasions without the most crippling embarrassments. They go hot all over, avoid the company (if they can) of the people who witnessed their stupidity, and suppose that these others recall the silly thing as often and as contemptuously as they do themselves.

Forget it! There was no evil intention. All of us have slipped in this way on some occasion or other. Put it behind you, and put it behind you *now*.

2. Secondly, I want you to forget your sins. We all have sins to repent. Have you been forgiven for them? Have you been to God about them in repentance—repentance lasting and deep? Have you made what restitution you could? Have you forsaken those sins, and are you living in the white light of God? Have you learned the lesson that folly was able to teach? Can you say "Yes" to all these questions? "I *am* repentant. I have been forgiven. I have made restitution. I have forsaken my sin. I have learned the lesson." The answer to every question is "Yes."

Be particularly sure about the restitution. Restitution isn't always possible and, where it is, it does not, of itself, wipe out the sin, but it helps forgetfulness. No man should hope to forget the wrong things he's done until he has done whatever he can to put them right. A false statement can be corrected. Hurt feelings can be healed by honest apologies. To do everything you can to make amends helps your misdeeds into oblivion. A gnawing conscience keeps the memory terribly alert!

But if the honest answer to all the questions is "Yes," then forget it!

Forget it! Throw it behind you. What does God say to a repentant people? 'I will forgive their iniquity, and their sin will I remember no more.' "*Their sin will I remember no more!*"

You are facing the future. There is need that you muster all the courage and hope that you can. Let the forgiveness of God cleanse all the pus out of that old wound and carry you forward with the light step of a forgiven man.

Paul had a past. The blood of the martyrs was on his hands,

but he went to God for forgiveness. And when he faced the future, he said, "Forgetting the things that are behind . . . and reaching forward to the things which are before, I press toward the mark."

Be right with God, and then forget the things which are behind you, and press forward toward the mark.

3. But there is something else I want you to forget besides your gaucheries and your sins. I want you to forget the hurtful things that have been done against you. In the Lord's Prayer we say, "Forgive us our trespasses as we forgive those who trespass against us." You need forgiveness yourself. "With what measure ye mete it shall be measured to you again." I want you to forget the sins of those who have sinned against you.

Have you been sinned against? Has somebody slandered you or done you the deepest injury? Are you nursing the hope of revenge in your heart?

Forget it! For your own sake and God's sake, cast it out of your heart now. However justified your resentment against another person may be, to harbor that resentment is to poison yourself. Be rid of that poison!

If it seems easy for me to say this, remember that I realize how hard it must be for some of you to do it. Indeed, I realize that you can't do it alone. "This kind cometh not out but by prayer." Only by the special help of God can you deal with those deep resentments.

But the help is available. Claim the help now! From every bit of the memory of it which is damaging for you to recall, ask God, in his mercy, to make you forget.

III

But how? How can one forget?

Isn't it asking the unreasonable about some major experience

31

of life which has been as gall and bitterness to us, simply to say "Forget." One can't forget at will. The changed circumstances that the fact has caused shriek aloud with every day as it comes. Can a deserted wife, left to struggle alone with her brood of young children, be expected to forget the deep disloyalty which has darkened all her days?

One cannot forget the *fact*. I have admitted so much. It is the bitterness and the emotional overwhelming from which deliverance may be obtained.

This is what I advise: *Remember to forget*.

Does that sound mad? But I mean it. Remember to forget!

If you think my psychology is all upside down, let me remind you that Immanuel Kant—a foremost philosophical figure of all time—uses that very phrase in his journal. Who could justly accuse *him* of being a shallow psychologist?

Kant never married, and lived for years in entire and trustful dependence on his manservant, Lampe. Then he discovered that Lampe had systematically robbed him, and he felt compelled to dismiss his old servant. But what a difference it made to his life! At every turn he missed the man he'd trusted and who had betrayed his trust. In his journal this pathetic line appears: "Remember to forget Lampe."

It is not Kant's forgiveness (or lack of it) I am discussing now, only his psychology.

You can remember to forget. You do it by reversing the process of remembering to remember.

To remember, one must revive the image, hold it in the mind for so long, revive it again—and regularly, and then it's there for good.

Reverse that process. *Don't* revive the image. When it rises of itself, summoned by some association of ideas (as it will), remember at once that this is something you remember to forget.

Turn the mind from it immediately. Have in the antechamber of your mind a few interesting themes always "on call"—your sports, hobbies, ambitions, holiday plans. Summon one of those topics instantly. The mind, like nature, abhors a vacuum. Think of this other absorbing theme.

None of these substitute themes is of any use unless it has power to grip the mind, and what grips one mind may not grip another. A friend of mine, a shy soul, outwits the recollection of a public gaucherie by instantly remembering an occasion when he was a social success. I know another man who blots out unwanted memories by trying to write a poem and another who dreams about the professional advancement he believes he will achieve some day. It does not matter what the substitute image is, so long as it is wholesome and can thrust the other thing from your attention. Prayer will not do if it is prayer *about the thing itself*. That keeps it *in* the memory. But prayer is *best of all* when it opens you to love, forgiveness, peace, and poise.

Less and less will the rejected image rise. Fewer and fewer will be its associations in your mind. When it does recur, it will be as a *fact* only; the emotions will not be in heat with it. It will be a cold fact or, at most, a tepid one. With the help of God you have remembered to forget what it was damaging to remember.

Let me stress, as I conclude, that it is only with the help of God that you can expect to succeed. Psychology alone is not enough. Be as clear as Joseph was that in this high enterprise it is God who makes us forget.

When the memory of your sin returns—be it but for the barest instant—do not dwell on it, not even in penitence. Dwell on the opposite—in longing and in prayer.

When the memory of those who have injured you returns, don't dwell on the injuries. Pray for those who have injured you.

It will insulate you from the harm their thoughts might still do to you, and it will keep the poison out of your own soul.

And if you still think that what I am asking is impossible—even with the help of God—suffer me to finish with a simple reminiscence.

It was Christmas time in my home. One of my guests had come a couple of days early and saw me sending off the last of my Christmas cards. He was startled to see a certain name and address. "Surely, you are not sending a greeting to *him*," he said.

"Why not?" I asked.

"But you remember," he began, "eighteen months ago . . ."

I remembered, then, the thing the man had publicly said about me, but I remembered also resolving at the time, with God's help, that I would remember to forget. And God had "made" me forget!

I posted the card.

3

Christ Has Double Vision

Jesus looked upon him, and said, Thou art Simon the
Son of John: thou shalt be called "Rock."—John 1:42

WHOM DO WE MEAN WHEN WE SAY "I"? IN THESE HUMAN
personalities of ours is there anything so constant, so integrated
and whole, that I can honestly refer to it as "I"? Common human
nature is changeful human nature, subject to swiftly alternating
moods, a mingling of shine and shade like an April day.

Who is the real man? The man who sings heartily in church
on Sunday mornings and feels all good inside, or the same man
when he grumbles at the breakfast table and makes a fearful
fuss over a bit of burnt toast? Is he the man of whom the office
boy at work is half afraid and concerning whom the typists
anxiously inquire, "What kind of mood is he in this morning?"
Or the same man when, at a Christmas party, he puts on a paper
cap and prances about like a schoolboy?

Who is the real man?

Who is the real woman?

Is she the person who did not go to bed for three weeks when
her child was ill and fought for his life with the tenacity of self-
less love? Or the same woman when, with thoughtless idle gos-
sip, she lightly took someone's character away? Is she the woman
who would go to any length to help a neighbor in serious trouble,

or the same woman who, with acid tongue, spoke with criticism of someone she unreasonably disliked? Who is the real woman? The same person can be such different persons. Whom do others mean when they say "you," and whom do you mean yourself when you say "I"?

Aristotle said that there were six different Aristotles. Faust said, "Two souls, alas, dwell in this breast of mine." Renan, the French author, said, "I am double. One part of me laughs while the other part cries." Paul speaks of "another self" dwelling within him. Even the nonphilosophic feel this dilemma at times. A working man once said to me, "They tell me to make up my mind. It would be easy if I only had one mind to make up, but I am in three minds about this thing."

When we get extreme instances of this dilemma, we talk of "schizophrenia" and "dual personality," but the rudiments of that trouble are in us all. The problem is real and practical, and, for spiritual purposes, I want to examine it now.

Let me begin to examine it in scripture. Let me begin with Simon, the Galilean fisherman, the brother of Andrew, and the son of John.

How many Simons were there?—three, at least.

1. There was Simon as his friends saw him.

2. There was Simon as he saw himself.

3. There was Simon as Christ saw him.

Let us look at each of them in turn.

I

1. What was Simon like as his friends saw him?

Oh, he was bluff, with qualities of leadership, impulsive both in anger and generosity, a blusterer at times, and at times loud-mouthed and dirty-mouthed—he could curse and swear with the worst of them.

Yet he had a way of being the outstanding person in the company, and what he did others so often did as well. He suffered the defects of the impulsive and proved at times unstable, but he was born to lead and could never be overlooked.

2. What was Simon like as he saw himself?

Not the same man that his friends saw! We never see ourselves as others see us. However much we offer the prayer of Robert Burns—

> Oh wad some power the giftie gie us
> To see oursels as others see us!

it is never answered—*except, of course, in an hour of spiritual revelation.*

We do not see ourselves as others see us physically. When we look in a mirror, we always see ourselves the wrong way round. And mentally and spiritually, it is always another self we see from within.

It is true in achievement. Others judge us by what we have done. We judge ourselves by what we feel we can do.

It is true with our faults. Except by special revelation, we never see our own faults clearly; the dark marks upon us, which are so plain to other people, seem hidden to our view. We see the faults plainly *in others* but not plainly in ourselves.

I went to a branch of a children's home some years ago. I spoke to the gracious sister in charge and asked if all the children in her branch had a foster aunt and uncle—the kind of people who, without adopting the child, write them letters, knit for them, and befriend them in the way that orphan and unwanted children so urgently need.

She said that all the children in the branch had such a friend except two, and one of the two was a little colored boy.

We met him. He was nearly four. His name was Philip. He

was the only colored boy in the home and beautifully black. But we were amused when Sister told us this story. The chimney sweep called one day, and Philip ran into the home in great alarm, buried his face in Sister's apron, and cried, "Oh, Sister, I'm frightened; there's a black man coming." No sweep was ever so black as Philip (who is a splendid young man now), but he had borrowed the talk of the other children, I suppose, and he didn't see much of himself then! Everybody else he saw was white.

That is a parable. It is the darkness in others we see and not in ourselves.

I think it was like that with Simon. His picture of himself, I imagine, was a flattering one. I believe that he thought himself to be a good judge of other people. He supposed himself to be— and, no doubt, it was partly true—a kind man, ready to do a good turn to everyone. He probably counted himself a good husband. No doubt he thought himself a good son-in-law, and we all know how concerned he was later when his mother-in-law was ill.

He probably judged himself to be loyal to his friends, good at his work, and quite a decent fellow.

It was an idealist picture, no doubt. If you had said to him, "Are you without faults?" he would, I imagine, have laughed at the idea.

"Oh, I have faults," he would have said. But he didn't particularize them. People don't until they are serious in the pursuit of holiness. He hadn't dug them out separately, itemized them to himself, prayed over them, and said, "This, and this, and this, is sin in me."

I once lived in the same house as an old lady whose favorite phrase was this: "I have many faults, but *that* isn't one of them."

In the passing of a month I believe she mentioned every sin

that flesh is heir to, asserting again, "I have many faults, but *that* isn't one of them."

If you would be serious with your faults, you must loathe them in your mind; you need to spread them out before God. Most of us carry an idealist picture of ourselves or one, at least, insufficiently frank about our faults. I think it was like that with Simon.

3. Finally, there was the Simon whom Christ saw. I think, if we were speaking with fullness as well as with accuracy, we should be obliged to say that our Lord saw two Simons. First, Simon as he was (which was neither the Simon his friends saw, nor the Simon he himself saw), the real man then existing, and, secondly, and more importantly, the Simon Christ could make him.

The two were so different that they required a different name. Our Lord, looking at Simon as he was, said, "Thou art Simon, the son of John," and then, looking at the Simon he could make, said, "Thou shalt be called 'Rock.' That is the man I'll make you."

What a change! The unstable can become a rock. The impulsive blusterer can be clear in judgment and firm in will. The man who could curse and swear and deny all knowledge of his best friend to save his own skin will become the valiant leader at Pentecost, the fearless and unshaken champion of the sect which was itself to shake the world.

The same man.

Who was the real man—Simon as his friends saw him, Simon as he saw himself, Simon as Jesus saw him?

II

1. Who is the real you? Is it the person your friends see?

I wonder what your friends really think about you? If you are rich, or in a position of authority, you may have very little idea what other people really think about you. Folk fawn on wealth and hide their true opinion from authority. Cupidity and a sense of security encourage them to do so. You may think that they regard you as a great fellow. But I wonder what they *really* think.

I knew a businessman once who was constantly speaking to me of the immense affection in which his workers held him. It always embarrassed me. I had positive knowledge that his workers loathed him. I didn't care to tell him so. I was not his minister, nor yet his intimate friend, and I knew that it would have been a terrible shock. But it was a fact. They loathed him in the office, and they loathed him in the warehouse, and they loathed him in the factory. They loathed him, most of all, when he made one of his periodic religious speeches.

I wonder what people really think about you?

Does it bother you that you might be an object of some contempt or mild amusement or deep dislike?

It needn't bother you—or not much! Listen! What matters to you and me, at the last, is not what other people think about us—though it would be interesting to know *why* they think as they do—but what *God* thinks about us.

2. Who is the real you? Is it the person you see yourself?

No! Positively no!

Unless your powers of introspection are heightened by a special revelation from God, you do not know yourself. Psychology alone is not enough. It is amazing how ignorant psychiatrists can be of themselves and how much some of them need the treatment they give to other people.

I doubt whether anybody really knows himself until he sees himself in the white light of God.

You remember the remark of the pygmy in the heart of Africa

when the first missionaries arrived. He said, "I didn't know I was black until the white men came."

We do not know the stains on our own life until we really see ourselves in the white light of God. But then we know, and how hard it is to bear!

No wonder Charles Wesley sang:

> Show me, as my soul can bear,
> The depth of inbred sin.

A bit at a time, Lord. More would be too much.

3. Who is the real you?

It is an act of faith, but I am ready to assert that the real you is the self which Christ could make you.

You were not made to grovel. You were not built to abide in sin. God made you for himself, and deep-seated in your heart there are longings after holiness. Every now and then the Spirit inflames them, and you long for the great spaces in which the saint moves.

I was in the zoo some time ago and lingered by the cages of the eagles. Somehow or other the sight of them hurt me. I looked at the great wingspread of the king of birds, and I felt sick at heart that they were caged. If only it were possible to make friends with the birds and the beasts and not rob them of their liberty. Made for the skies—and crammed in a cage!

So many of us are like that: made for the skies and imprisoned in sin.

When Jesus looks at us, he sees us as we are, but, with his double vision, he sees us also as we might be.

He looked on Simon and saw Peter. He looked on Saul and saw Paul. He looked on Augustine the roué and saw Augustine the saint. When he looks on you, he sees you, maybe ineffective, inferior, frustrated, beaten by beastliness. He sees you as you are, but he sees you also dependable, confident, effective, sanctified.

If we could only see ourselves as Christ sees us! If we could stand at his elbow and get that double vision; the men and women we are; the men and women we *might* be!

Emerson said:

> Could'st thou in vision see
> Thyself the man God meant,
> Thou never more could'st be
> The man that art content.

See yourself then "the man God meant." Hold the picture in the eye of reverent imagination whenever you pray. Dwell (on your knees) on the thought that God could make you like *that*, and, as you dwell upon it daily and in prayer, God will use your sanctified imagination to pull you up. The actual will turn into the ideal. The difference may be so marked that you will need a new name. To you as to one long ago, he may say, "Thou art Simon . . . thou shalt be called 'Rock.'"

4

Holy—but Stained!

Aaron shall bear iniquity of the holy things.
—Exod. 28:38

WHAT AN ODD PHRASE! "THE INIQUITY OF THE HOLY THINGS."
Whatever does it mean?

The religion of the Hebrews—deep in a wisdom we often overlook—provided not only for forgiveness for the plain wickedness of the people when they were penitent, but forgiveness also for the stains which sometimes disfigured holy things.

For instance it was required of the devout Jew that he tithe himself for the work of God, but the tithe estimate could be faked like a modern income-tax return. *That* was iniquity upon a holy thing. It was required of a devout Jew that he make periodic sacrifices to God, and, always, it had to be an unblemished sacrifice: a lamb without spot, a pair of perfect pigeons, a couple of lovely doves. Theoretically, it was to be "the utmost for the highest." In point of fact it was often the least for the highest: the lamb that was ailing, anyhow, a pair of scruffy pigeons which the dealer knocked off cheap. The last book of the Old Testament deals not with lofty moral themes but largely with these shabby subterfuges of a people outwardly religious but grudging in their heart, and the Aaronic priesthood had, as one of its functions, to intercede with God not only for the sins of the people, but for the affectations in their holiness as well.

Is there any need for such a service on our behalf? Are we guilty of iniquity in holy things?

I think we are.

Let me show you what I have in mind.

I

There is, first, our *penitence*. Penitence is a holy thing. It is in penitence that we first come to almighty God. All serious dealing with God begins on the human side, in penitence. We have erred and strayed from his ways like lost sheep. We have followed too much the devices and desires of our own heart. We have offended against his holy laws. We have all sinned and come short of the glory of God. We cannot hope to restore the relationship except as we begin with penitence.

But our penitence is sometimes a shabby thing. Wasn't it George Whitefield who said, "Our repentance needs to be repented of, and our tears washed in the blood of Christ"?

"But what," you may ask, "can be wrong with penitence? What in it can possibly need to be washed in the blood of Christ?"

Sometimes our repentance is not real repentance at all; it is only remorse and fear. Sometimes we are sad and even in tears, not because we have done wrong, but because we have been found out or may yet be found out.

Here is a youth who comes to me in trouble. He has embezzled his employer's money, and his employer has found out. At any time the prosecution will begin.

So I go to the employer and plead with him to be merciful, tell him that there are ways in which the money can be restored and the youth can be saved, explain that this is breaking the heart of the boy's good parents, urge him to overlook the thing.

And he relents, accepts the money back, and calls the prosecution off.

When I have it all tidied up and tell the young man, to my amazement all his distress disappears in a moment. He smiles. He laughs. There's nothing left to worry about. All is well now. He seems to think it was a pity the money had to be paid back.

He isn't sorry for his sins at all. He is only sorry for the price he thought he had to pay.

Here is a girl who comes to me in anguish because, though unwed, she fears that she is to have a child. I talk to her as a minister may. I do all for her that I can in that miserable time and plan for the future too.

And then she realizes that she is *not* to have a child after all, and immediately all her distress departs. She is bright. She is gay. What was she worrying about, anyhow?

We realize it then. This is not repentance for sin. This is only fear and passing remorse, a shabby counterfeit. Her very penitence needs to be repented of and her tears washed in the blood of Christ.

But let me be on guard against feeling superior to these sinners. Hasn't my penitence been spurious at times? Have I been sorry, not because I have offended God, but because I have lost my inner peace or found my spirit clouded or missed the sweets of communion with heaven? Am I cast down, not because I have offended against his holy laws, but because I have suffered some personal deprivations? This is not true repentance. There is an iniquity upon the holy thing.

II

Think, in the second place, of *worship*. Worship is a holy thing. What does a forgiven soul most want to do—*to worship and adore the great, forgiving God!* Worship is a holy thing, but, alas, there is often a stain upon it.

We come to worship and find our minds distracted by the interests and cares of the world, not the great solemn cares which demand to be brought into the presence of God, but petty, mean, and groveling things; not care about a wayward child, which might well oppress your mind even in the sanctuary, but ludicrous things like the shape of Mrs. So-and-so's hat or the impression you made at her party or what that nice boy thinks about you! These are more of the iniquities of the holy things.

Men who attempt the hard task of teaching others how to think say that a great deal of our everyday mental life is taken up by fantasy-thinking. Fantasy-thinking is a kind of daydreaming in which the mind wanders unchecked where it will, but where the emotions of fear and hope have more to do with it than any honest grappling with realities. A cartoonist illustrated that tendency recently by a picture of people waiting for a bus. They were ordinary enough people to look at, and they were all doing the same thing in this prosaic world—waiting for a bus—but over the head of every one of them the artist had drawn, in a kind of balloon, what their fantasy-thinking was at that moment. A little girl was at the head of the line, being held firmly by the hand of a forbidding nurse. In her fantasy the little girl was chasing the nurse with a big stick. A horsy man was reading the racing page of a newspaper and studying the starters and prices; in his fantasy-thinking he could see his horse winning and a pile of bills and coins was flooding over him. A girl was next in the line pulling off her gloves; in her fantasy-thinking she was Juliet on the balcony and Romeo was aspiring to her. So it went on.

You are not in a bus line; you are in church. Is your mind in church? Your heart? If it be true that God knows the thoughts of our mind—and he does—what does he see in that balloon over our heads when we are ostensibly at worship but really allowing our thoughts to drift unchecked where they will? Concentration and consecration are closer than you know. We need more concentration in worship. We need help to redeem the iniquity of the holy thing.

III

And think of our prayers. Surely prayer is a holy occupation. Coleridge said that "prayer is the highest activity of which the human soul is capable," and, at its best, he was right. But it isn't always at its best. Our prayers are sometimes scamped and often selfish. Some professing Christians go for days and do not pray at all, or leave it till the end of the day and fall asleep over it, or only pray with strength and desire when they want something for themselves.

Think of it. They go to the altar, and they are still selfish in the holy place. They draw nigh to God, and when they have the ear of the Almighty, they do not plead for some poor soul they know to be in great trouble, but they take all the time over some petty thing their selfish heart is set upon. Is that an iniquity of the holy thing? Is that a stain on what should be most sacred?

Perhaps we are all guilty here to some extent? Is there one among us who will deny that when his child was ill or his wife in danger, his business in peril, or his own health uncertain, he achieved a passion in prayer he had never reached before?

And how strange that, with the memory of that experience in mind, it doesn't quicken all his impulse to intercession, and when he hears of someone else in grave trouble, does not say within his soul, "I have been there and I remember. I will go to God for him, and if importunity and pleading will get the blessing, I mean to have it."

Alas! the ranks of the real intercessors are thin. Prayer with many Christians, I say, is scant and selfish. It is an iniquity upon a holy thing.

IV

Think, then, of our *service*. Most of us recognize the obligation to do some regular and unpaid service for God. We recognize, I hope, the obligation to do our *normal daily work* for God, but, in addition, we feel privileged to do extra things for him: sing in a choir, serve in some office in his Church, engage in youth or social welfare work, keep God's accounts for him, and a hundred other services he condescends to receive at our hands.

What an unspeakable privilege to be allowed to do anything for God at all! Fancy being accepted into his service and "put upon the strength," actually allowed—with the unaffected brightness of a Christian—to wear his livery and call oneself by his name.

Years ago, when I lived in Sussex, I was invited, on one occasion, by the Duchess of Norfolk to Arundel Castle for an evening of chamber music. It was in aid of some charity, I think, and I went with delight.

Unhappily, I went in at the wrong door and missed my way in the vast labyrinth of buildings. The chamber music was to be in the Baron's Hall, but I went up and down and round and couldn't find the Baron's Hall. Then I spied a lady who seemed to know the place well, and when I told her my difficulty, she kindly took me there herself.

"This is the Baron's Hall," she said, as we arrived, and when I thanked her, she nicely brushed my thanks aside and said, with a touch of pride, "I am happy to do it. I am her Grace's personal servant."

We can say even more. The King of kings and Lord of lords and Only Ruler of princes accepts us as his personal servants.

Isn't it the more shameful, therefore, that our service is at times unworthy and that we are not always eager, happy, and conscious of the privilege of being allowed to do it?

Some of us neglect it or do it just by half; some are peeved when they aren't praised by other people, and still more peeved when someone else is praised in their place! It was reward enough to be allowed to serve, but here we are, thrusting ourselves forward, when all the glory belongs by right to him, and our service to God is spoiled by our thirst for personal praise.

Is that an iniquity of the holy thing? I am compelled to regard it as such.

God have mercy upon us!

You will hardly credit the truth of this incident, but I know the facts, and I know where it occurred.

A certain church choir was giving a special week-night performance in a town hall in aid of a civic fund. It was discovered, at the last moment, that the platform at the town hall wasn't high enough, and another low platform had to be placed hastily upon the first. It was not as large as the platform proper and left the choir on two levels. Some of the singers, therefore, were obliged to stand lower than the others all the evening, and one lady took umbrage at this. She hasn't been to the choir since, and it occurred six months ago!

I think now that she feels the foolishness of it herself, but pride complicates the matter, and she cannot swallow it enough to go back.

So she is out of the Royal Service, miserable in her own heart, and small in the judgment of others, all over the level of a platform!

Don't feel too superior as I tell the story. Don't say, "I would never do that!" (Maybe you couldn't get into a choir anyway!) Search your own heart. It may be that upon your service there has fallen at times a shadow no less disfiguring, and you have been guilty also of an iniquity upon the holy thing.

V

Think, finally, of our giving. It is one of the loveliest things God ever does to us mortals when he condescends to take our gifts. He knows how the swelling heart loves to give, and he royally stoops to take. He doesn't say, as the great ones of this earth might, "You can't give to me; there is nothing you have that I want." He takes what we give, our money among other things, and he puts it to holy use.

Isn't it all the more amazing, therefore, that we should be mean in our giving to God and bring, like the Hebrews whom Malachi condemned, a blemished sacrifice to the altar—less than we should and grudging at that?

Few Christians would deny that people may legitimately spend some of their earnings on wholesome pleasure, but should there not be a proportion between what we spend on pleasure and what we give to God? Surely, it ought not be more on my personal pleasure than I give to the work of my Master.

What do I spend, then, on pleasure? If I smoke, how much goes in smoking? If I visit the movies or the theatre, what do I pay then? What does my sport cost me or my recreational books? What does the car cost, when I use it only for a jaunt? And now, on the other side, what do I give to God?

Can you abide that questioning? Can you pass the test of your own conscience? If what we give to God is stored up for us above, how well off will we be in heaven?

I heard a wealthy and ungenerous man say once that he knew he didn't give much to the work of God, but that he meant to leave a lot of money for that purpose when he died.

It impressed me less than he thought it ought. It sounded as though he were saying, "God can have it when I can use it no more."

Are there things about your giving you are ashamed to remember? Is there even an iniquity on the holy thing? Is there something in it which needs to be forgiven. Did you ever seriously consider tithing? Have you been mean with the Almighty who has been so generous with you?

There then is our condemnation. There is something to be forgiven in the best things we ever do.

Who will undertake for us?

We understand the phrase clearly. It had meaning for the Hebrews, and it has meaning for us also. In our penitence, in our worship, in our prayer, in our service, in our giving, we are under the condemnation of our consciences.

Nor can the Aaronic priesthood avail for us.

> Not all the blood of beasts
> On Jewish altars slain
> Could give the guilty conscience peace
> Or wash away our stain.
>
> But Christ, the heavenly Lamb,
> Takes all our sins away.

A greater than Aaron comes to our aid. Ah! that's the wonderful truth. Where we went with our vicious sins, we must go with our soiled virtues. There is hope for us only at Calvary.

Bundle them together: our impenitent penitence, our unworthy worship, our poor, selfish, and uncompassionate prayer, our praise-seeking service, and our ungenerous giving.

O God—and to think that we used to be proud of ourselves! Up the sacred hill we go.

Coming, as at first we came,
To take, and not bestow on Thee.

Lord! Lord! Forgive! We are unprofitable servants—so unprofitable, indeed, that we have even felt good at times, good on our own and good by our giving, serving, praying. We know the truth now. Save us! Save us from our "goodness!" Thou has sprinkled our sins. Sprinkle our virtues too!

And all the gifts we bring,
And all the vows we make,
And all the acts of love
We plan for Thy dear sake,
Into Thy pardoning thought
O God of mercy, take.

5

The Homesickness of the Soul

At home with the Lord—II Cor. 5:8

ALL STUDENTS OF NATURAL HISTORY KNOW OF THE WONDERFUL instinct of direction displayed by birds, beasts, and fish. It is sometimes called "the homing instinct."

Cats and dogs often find their way back across wide stretches of unknown country. Pigeons fly direct to their homes hundreds of miles away. Sea birds carried round the coast from one side of England to the other return unerringly (apparently straight over the land) to the very cliff or burrow from which they were removed. Swallows, and other migrant birds, take a confident aerial journey between destinations thousands of miles apart. Salmon return to spawn in the rivers of their birth. Young eels steer their way through a wide heaving ocean to hereditary waters which they have never seen. Nothing in all nature is more wonderful than this amazing instinct of the lower creation for home.

The question has sometimes been raised whether or not man ever possessed this same homing instinct and lost it through the ages in his preoccupation with other things. The query is usually waived aside either with a direct negative or by the assertion that the evidence is too slight for an answer to be given.

I want to raise the question again. There is a deeper answer to it than most enquirers have guessed, a *spiritual* answer. Deep in the heart of man there is a homing instinct, profound, persistent, ineradicable, which he often ignores and might even deny, but which, if he turned his attention to it, might make him realize the inwardness of a line in the hymnbook at which, in other moods, he would be openly amused: "*Heaven is my home.*"

I am aware, as I begin, that some among you will deny the very idea of it, but I base my argument on two undeniable facts of human nature, and, if you resist my inference at the end, you have still to explain those facts in some other way.

I

I want to lay it down, first, as quite incontrovertible that *there is something in man which earth can never satisfy*. It is common for people to say and to believe that if they only had this or that coveted thing they would always be happy, and some of them die believing it. But the evidence of those who obtain the "treasure" does not bear them out. It satisfied for a little while, and then there was the old, persistent hunger again, clamorous as ever.

No one will deny that to lack money to meet the simple needs of life is to miss happiness, but it is a widespread error to suppose that a lot of money means a lot of joy. Jay Gould, the famous American millionaire who died possessing fifty million dollars, summed up his life (not in a mood of despondency) but as his wrought-out and considered verdict on himself) in these words: "I suppose I am the most miserable devil on earth."

Some people set their mind on a coveted position and believe that complete satisfaction for them would come by its achievement; they work and scheme and plan to obtain that high post, but the satisfaction of arriving soon fades. When Benjamin Disraeli, twice Prime Minister of England, reviewed his life, he said, "Youth is a mistake; manhood a struggle; old age a regret." He may have been posing again, but men who could never be accused as *poseurs* have echoed his words.

Fame is the will-o'-the-wisp which beckons others on. Milton, you will remember, called fame "that last infirmity of noble mind." Sir Walter Scott achieved it—great and worthy and deserved fame—but there was that in him which not all the praise of men could satisfy. When dying he said, "Bring me the book."

"The book?" they said. "What book?"

"There is only one book," he answered a little wearily. "Bring me the Bible."

Pleasure is the goal of other people. Its pursuit becomes a science with them. The art of life, as they conceive it, is to squeeze from every moment the utmost pleasure it will yield, but so often it turns to gall and bitterness at the last. Byron may be taken as typical of the grosser hedonists. He drifted, in the quest of pleasure, from one woman to another, and died an old man at thirty-six, saying of himself on his last birthday:

> My days are in the yellow leaf;
>   The flowers and fruits of love are gone;
> The worm, the canker, and the grief
>   Are mine alone!

Some people pursue physical health; indeed, cults have grown up which make the fitness of this human form the end of all striving. But there are spiritual maladies which no harmony of the body can really cure and which, if uncured, will rob the body of its health as well.

I lived in a town once where there also lived a doctor who had forsaken normal medical practice in order to advise people on how not to be ill and who was himself such a picture of physical fitness that folk came from miles around to consult him about health. But I remember also the morning he came early to my door in agony of heart to tell of a deep malady in his own soiled soul and to ask my advice upon a moral problem which was grave indeed.

Now, that is my first point. There is something in man which earth cannot satisfy, not even the best things of earth. The testimony of those who have achieved coveted things is emphatic and uniform; there still remains a longing and a hunger and a heartache which nothing material or terrestrial seems able to meet. We live on earth and yet, somehow, we do not *belong* to it. In certain ways we have kinship with the beasts, but, so far as we can judge, earth satisfies them.

> Irks care the crop-full bird?
> Frets doubt the maw-crammed beast?

Earth does not satisfy us I cannot help feeling that that is an impressive fact. I warn you against supposing that if only you had more of this or more of that, you would be completely satisfied. It is an illusion. Earth *cannot* satisfy you. William Watson—in his poem "World-Strangeness"—asked:

> In this house with starry dome,
> Floored with gemlike plains and seas,
> Shall I never feel at home,
> Never wholly be at ease? [1]

Never! You weren't meant to.

II

Here is a second fact. I believe that *there is in man a nostalgia for Heaven.* Forgive me for reminding you that the words "nostalgia" comes from two Greek words: "nostos," meaning "return home," and "algos," meaning "pain." It meant originally home-

[1] Used by permission of George G. Harrap and Co., Ltd.

sickness as an incurable malady, incurable by anything—except, of course, *by home.*

Now, I believe that although it is hidden, ignored, overlaid, and even denied, there is in man a homesickness for heaven. Wordsworth, in his famous ode on "Intimations of Immortality from Recollections of Early Childhood," speaks with plainness of this secret reminiscence in the soul. He says:

> Our birth is but a sleep and a forgetting:
> The Soul that rises with us, our life's Star,
>   Hath had elsewhere its setting,
>   And cometh from afar:
>   Not in entire forgetfulness,
>   And not in utter nakedness,
> But trailing clouds of glory do we come
> From God, Who is our home.

"From God, Who is our home."

All that Wordsworth had in mind when he said that is beyond the range of our present interest, but I *do* believe that there is in man a homesickness for heaven, that that ache which earth cannot satisfy can be satisfied by God, that all feel it, but only some understand it, that in a deeper sense than Cleopatra meant we might each truly say, "I have immortal longings in me."

There is an old legend of the Western Isles concerning a sea king who desired the company of a human being. One day he heard in his cavern under the sea a cry, a little human cry, and rose to the surface of the water to discover a child in a derelict boat. Just as he was about to make for the little vessel and take the child, a rescue party intervened, and he missed his prize. But, so the legend says, as they drew away with the one so nearly lost, the sea king cupped his hand and threw into the heart of the child a little sea-salt wave and said, as he submerged, "The child is mine. When it grows, the salt sea will call him and he will come home to me at the last."

It is only a Gaelic legend, but it enshrines the timeless truth. God has put in the heart of everyone of us a longing for himself. The mass of men do not understand it. They just know that there are times when they want to be quiet, times when they want to be alone, times when the calendar, the stars, or death speaks to them. They *hunger* and they *thirst*—but for what?

It is part of the service of religion to make the hunger of our souls clear to us, and that is why this nostalgia is known in its true meaning only among the devout. Our fathers sang:

> Strangers and pilgrims here below,
>   This earth, we know, is not our place;
> But hasten through the vale of woe,
>   And, restless to behold Thy face,
> Swift to our heavenly country move,
> Our everlasting home above.

And, as the song swelled and the certainty of self-understanding gripped their hearts, they burst into this glorious verse:

> Through Thee, who all our sins hast borne,
>   Freely and graciously forgiven,
> With songs to Zion we return,
>   Contending for our native heaven;
> That palace of our glorious King
> We find it nearer while we sing.

And will you notice this? If you have spiritual discernment, whenever you meet a saint, you become aware of two things about him. At one moment you feel "how natural and at home he is," and the next you say to yourself, "The man is an exile; he doesn't belong here at all."

You notice it in Paul. How busy he is for the Kingdom in affairs of this world, and then he sighs in my text to be "at home with the Lord."

That was how they always felt about Thomas Erskine of Linlathen. A friend tells me that, after his death, his life recurred to the memory of his old acquaintances like "the sigh of an exile. He seemed never to take root in this world. To him, many of the things that most interested other men were only the furniture of an inn, not really important; he wasn't *staying*. He was a wayfarer—a pilgrim." That is one of the authentic marks of the saint. He is "the pilgrim of an inward Odyssey." This earth, he knows, is not his place.

My friends, do you know that? I want to say to any poor, lost sinner now: You may have lost your way, but don't lose your address. Don't deny that hunger in your soul. Don't say it isn't there; earth satisfies me; when this life is over, I will have had all that I want of life.

That, I notice, is what Logan Pearsall Smith says in his autobiography: "For any other form of being I feel no longing." He had lost the religion of his saintly mother. He never had a robust religion of his own. Then he denied the hunger for anything more. I say again, "He had not only lost his way; he had lost his address."

God keep you on your guard against that. The homesickness for God in your heart is a precious, divine gift. It won't make you less keen to serve your fellows here below, but it will be a constant reminder to you that the most permanent dwelling earth provides is a tent, and at any time the word may come to draw the pegs. We are, indeed, "strangers and pilgrims here below."

Your interest in heaven may expose you, of course, to the

charge—even from fellow Christians—of "otherworldliness." People who have made the "social gospel" the whole gospel are very free with that charge.

Ignore it!

You have been well taught that the interpretation of the Christian ethic in communal life is part of your plain business, but you know, and I know, that the only "new Jerusalem" we shall see is "not made with hands," but is "eternal in the heavens."

> Far o'er yon horizon
> Rise the City towers,
> Where our God abideth;
> That fair home is ours.

Here we sojourn; there we belong. You will work with zest and skill and thoroughness in all that concerns the outworkings of God's purpose on this earth, and you will work the better because, by faith, you have the perfect always in view.

Only those people work with full effectiveness for the new Jerusalem below who see the new Jerusalem above. They make it after "the pattern which has been shown them in the mount."

Think of the glorious social consequences of the evangelistic work of John Wesley and Lord Shaftesbury and William Booth —all God-intoxicated men, all consciously marching to Zion, all sure of heaven.

Be sure of it yourself; it is where you *belong*.

> Send hope before to grasp it,
> Till hope be lost in sight.

Some time ago a poor drunkard came into my church and committed his life to Christ. Twenty years before he had been a church official, but he came to London, took to drink, and drifted to the gutter. When he capitulated to Christ, he had a pathetic hope that his thirst might be quenched by some stroke of omnipotence.

It wasn't.

There began on that day, when he surrendered to our Lord, a long guerrilla warfare in his soul between the deadly craving and the keeping power of Christ.

As his new friend I suggested that, on any day in which he found the fight especially hard, he might drop in, and we could have a prayer together. He dropped in quite often. His drawn face often told its own story. We would go into the little chapel at once and pray.

One day, as I was praying with him, he broke down completely. The contrast between his earlier life of holy service and the revolting bestiality to which drunkenness had brought him was too much. He sobbed like a child and said, "I know I'm in the gutter. I *know* it. But Oh! . . . I don't belong there, do I? Tell me, I don't belong there. . . ."

I put my arm around him. I felt a great elation even in the embarrassment of his tears. He had lost his way—but not his address.

"No," I said quite positively, "you don't belong there; you belong to God. At the last *heaven is your home.*"

6

Four Judgments on Jesus

Many of them said, He hath a demon—John 10:20
Some said, He is a good man—John 7:12
Simon Peter ... said, Thou art the Christ—Matt. 16:16
Thomas ... said, ... My Lord and my God.
                                        —John 20:28

THE HISTORIAN SAYS THAT OLIVER CROMWELL WAS EITHER HATED or loved. He was so strong a personality that he could not be ignored. Almost against their will he forced men to take up a forthright attitude toward him.

That is by no means peculiar to Cromwell. In its degree it is true of every strong personality (of a man like President Franklin D. Roosevelt in our own era), and it is true in a striking degree of Jesus. Men found it impossible to be indifferent to him. They might accept him or reject him; they might bless him or curse him; they might swear *by* him or swear *at* him. What they couldn't do was to neglect him. There was that in Jesus that would not be ignored.

Indeed, it is possible to group the men and women with whom Jesus came into contact according to the attitude they adopted toward him. They fall, not unnaturally, into three classes.

There were, first, his enemies. Drawn chiefly from the upper and professional classes, they said, "He hath a demon." They said also, "He hath a devil—and is mad." They said, "This man blasphemeth." They said also, "Behold, a gluttonous man and a wine-bibber!" They hated him. "He is a friend and agent of the devil," they said.

The second group was not less definite in its opinion. They said, "He is a good man." The suggestion that he was anything more than a man they would have set aside as fanciful and absurd. Nonetheless, they insisted on his goodness. The bereaved are consoled; the sick are cheered; the lonely find a friend; the poor have good tidings preached unto them. This is evidence they cannot gainsay. To all the foul insinuations of his enemies they turn a deaf ear. "No!" they say. "No! He is a good man."

The third group find its voice in Peter. It is a declaration born of experience and thought. It is the outcome of intimate contact and deep brooding. Doubtless, it was a profounder statement than Peter himself perceived in the moment of its utterance. "Thou art the Christ," he said, "the Son of the living God."

So we have an ascending scale.

"He hath a demon."

"He is a good man."

"He is the Christ."

Very simply, I want to thread my way along that upward path. I do not travel as a systematic theologian seeking the deep abstraction, nor yet as an encyclopedist, covetous of every scrap of evidence. I travel as a simple wayfaring man, pondering the reasons a wayfarer may. Frankly, I want to stand with Peter— or climb yet higher and say with Thomas, "My Lord and my God."

I cannot pretend to be unbiased or to set out on this quest without a particular hope in my heart. I live in a dark world. If I can be sure of Jesus, who he was and what he said, I can go forward unafraid. If I can be certain of him, I will dread nothing. Walk at my side now. Let us be sure what we think of Jesus Christ.

I

I will begin with those who say, "He hath a demon."

It is hard to believe that men ever accused Jesus of complicity with the Devil. It is not hard to believe that they thought him mad. The modern world has grave doubts still of his sanity. It is not hard to believe that they suspected him, on one occasion at least, of blasphemy; the orthodox Jew would be shocked at anybody who claimed to forgive sin.

But it is hard to believe that men ever accused Jesus of being in league with the Devil or of having a set determination to be vile. Only bitter hatred could have brought them to that.

To begin with, there was the evidence of his blameless life. "He went about doing good." He was free from crude ambition, exhibitionism, and common self-seeking. His chief interests were clearly spiritual. His sublime teaching about God and his uncanny knowledge of the human heart, both tell of a soul of the rarest quality. His own fierce condemnation of sin is burning in its intensity.

All this must have been clear to any discerning and unprejudiced man who met him in the days of his flesh.

Nor does the evidence end there.

From the hundred other reasons we could employ for rejecting this base slander, I will select one.

It is freely allowed that no man is a hero to his valet. The world may speak of him in superlative terms, but the servant who sees him at all odd hours—at night when he is overtired, in the morning before he is properly awake, when business overpresses, when disappointment comes, when he is off-guard and under no temptation to pose—this man does not normally think of his master as a hero. He knows the other side.

It is easily possible to know too much about some people. I remember from my college days that the head gardener never came to the college chapel when a student was planned to preach. He said, half in jest and half in earnest, "I know 'em. I grow 'em. I'm like the man who works at a jam factory; he has no taste for jam."

Who was it that first claimed that Jesus was sinless and used of him the awesome name of God?

The disciples! The men who had shared every kind of experience with him that mortals could share, who had seen him at all hours of day and night, who had seen him tired, hungry, and disappointed, scorned, abused, and hunted to death, who had ridden with him on a wave of popularity and hidden with him from inquisitive miracle-mongers, who had met him when he came down from a sleepless night of prayer on the hillside and known him physically overworked and emotionally overwrought. These were the men—eleven of them—who, with amazing unanimity, declared him, at the last, to be the sinless One.

It is an extraordinary testimony. To any unbiased mind it makes the charge of his enemies utterly false. Carlyle refused to believe in the insincerity of Mohammed in his early years for this chief reason; his employer and his slave, both of whom saw him daily and were each qualified, in their different ways, to discover hypocrisy in him, both believed in him with all their hearts.

No thinking man can doubt the quality of Christ's character—whatever theory he may hold as to his person—if he give attentive heed to the unanimous testimony of the men who knew him best.

II

Let us move on to the group who say, "He is a good man."

This is a perfectly understandable position. It is held by thousands of thoughtful people today. It is an attitude of mind which claims to be unprejudiced, to recognize facts, and is yet cautious in inference. "He is a good man," they say. "So much must be admitted. It cannot, indeed, be denied. But nothing more need be added. Leave it at that."

Well, if it is admitted that Jesus is a good man—and we have found it impossible to resist the inference—it will also be admitted, I think, that every good man has a sense of guilt. The better the man, the keener his sense of guilt. Good John Bunyan was so troubled about his sin that he wept and trembled and spent the nights, he tells us, "in sighs and tears." John Wesley, analyzing his experience prior to his conversion (and he had always lived, you remember, an exemplary life), says that he was in a "vile abject state of bondage to sin." The Apostle Paul uses language stronger still. He says, "I am the chief of sinners. I know that in me dwelleth no good thing." These men must not be understood as romancers; nor are they guilty of the "devil's darling sin"—the pride that apes humility. They were utterly sincere in these expressions of inward sin, even though, in their day, they might have passed as models of probity. It is, in short, an infallible mark of a good man that he has a keen sense of guilt. If we knew a man who, on our slight acquaintance, had impressed us as being a good man, and we heard him assert that he was without sin, we should be inclined, on that single fact alone, to revise our judgment of him.

Now, it is just here that another aspect of the uniqueness of Jesus emerges again. He was, by the unanimous testimony of most intimate witnesses, a good man, and yet he had no sense of

66

guilt. Publicly he made the challenge, "Which of you convicteth me of sin?"—and there was none to answer. Not only were his intimates unable to discover sin in him; he had no awareness of it himself. He lived intimately with his Father-God, but the holiness of God did not rebuke him.

We are face to face with something unique in human experience: a good man—without a sense of sin. Can we abide in the hypothesis of his mere manhood? If it be granted that he was good, and if it be granted that a good man always has a keen sense of sin, are we not constrained to believe that he was something more than a good man? Speaking for myself, I am so constrained. I cannot abide in the belief that he was a mere man. I sought to live in that faith once, but he outgrew the category. Does he not outgrow the category in your mind as well?

I do not suggest that the whole case rests on the one argument I have used, for that, by itself, is but a scrap of the evidence.

Yet it clearly points one way.

Let us follow the road it leads to and stand with Peter when he says, "Thou art the Christ."

III

No greater claim could be made for anyone. It is claimed for him that he is the Promised of Israel, the self-disclosure of God. Dare we join the company of those who stake that claim?

What might a plain man ask of such a claimant to these high and august titles? Might he ask a sign?

That is what the Jews asked from him: "Give us a sign," they said.

What did they mean?

They meant a wonder, a miracle, some astonishing physical phenomenon. "Give us a sign," they urged, and always he refused.

After all, what would a miracle prove for spirituality and deep religion? The credentials of God are not to be found in signs and wonders and portents. "An evil and adulterous generation," said Jesus, "seeketh after a sign . . . and no sign shall be given unto it."

And in any case we can't ask for such signs today.

What would be proof to us? How can we be sure that he was all that they claimed he was? We must know the answer to this. If he was the Christ of God, all his words are dependable. If he was just a good man, and sadly self-deceived in his claim to speak with authority, we are utterly without hope in this dark world, and God has never spoken unambiguously by anyone.

Well . . . here are half a dozen reasons which might make us uncomfortable in the supposition that he was just a good man.

He accepted worship—which is the right of God alone.

He forgave sins—which, again, is God's unique prerogative.

His personal claims drive us to one clear alternative: either that he was deranged, or he was all that he said he was. "I am the bread of life." "I am the light of the world." "No one cometh unto the Father, but by me." "The Son of man is lord of the sabbath." "He that loseth his life for my sake shall save it."

He has won devoted adherents—and in increasing multitudes —as century has succeeded century. Nearly a third of the world now acknowledges the carpenter as King. The witness of time is emphatically with him.

He has won devoted followers among all the races of men. Mohammed said that this Moslem religion would flourish where the palm tree grew, and, in the main, he was right. But no limit of clime or culture can be put to the sway of this Jesus. Negroes and Eskimos, Chinese and Chilean—all declare that Jesus is Lord. Geography emphatically witnesses to him.

Yet even that is not enough. Weighty as it is, the human heart craves, I think, for some *personal* proof.

Is it possible for us to have a personal proof?

I'm sure it is. At the last *the proof is in you.*

I mean *this.*

Every man or woman who *really* meets Jesus feels the impress and challenge of his life. There is something utterly unique in meeting him. Everybody who has had the experience—and a multitude of you have—is behind me in this assertion. When Christ looks at you, you know that he sees you through and through: your secret hopes, your nameless fears, your gusty passions, your dirty, furtive sins. You cannot pose to him.

Yet, when you see how truly he loves you, though he knows the worst about you, and "beckons you his road," all that is decent in you leaps out in response. Your heart cries out for him. You know it. You feel it. You would be lying if you denied that he pulled the heart out of you.

That's the proof you were seeking. He embodies all that you have "willed or hoped or dreamed of good." He does not need to display any other credentials. Your heart knows him, cries out to him, will not be satisfied without him.

Oh! you *can* run away from him like the rich young ruler did, but it is only your body that will run. Your heart will play you traitor. It knows its Lover and will abide with him. Having truly seen him once, it will hunger for him forever.

"None but Christ can *satisfy.*"

Though you live a whole long life through in willful rebellion and will not have this man to rule over you, nothing and no one else can give you peace.

Therefore, I say, if you would prove him, meet him. Open your heart to him. Fashion your lips in prayer. (It may be years since you prayed, and you may feel half-foolish as you do so now—but do it! It will take some of the stiff-necked pride out of you to come in penitence and petition to Christ.)

And—listen—he will make your heart burn within you, and he will stir in you longings after the noblest life.

IV

I come to my fourth text: Thomas said, "My Lord and my God."

I suggested earlier that when Peter said, "Thou art the Christ," it was a profounder statement than Peter himself perceived at the time. The twelve disciples were Jews to a man. They had been steeped in their high and ancient faith, and their belief in one God was as granite in their mind. "Hear, O Israel, the Lord our God is one Lord." *The Messiah*, the Promised One would come, they knew, but it is more than dubious that they ever expected God to come *in person* and as a working man. The fisherman of Galilee never pondered, I imagine, deep questions on the personality of the Deliverer. When Peter said, "Thou art the Christ," it would be wrong to infer that he had already glimpsed the Christian doctrine of Christ—much less the doctrine of the Holy Trinity!

It was Thomas who stepped nearer to the truth in the upper room. Christ had come back from the grave. He whom the winds and waves obeyed—conquered death also. Without understanding all he said, down on his knees went Thomas and spoke from the depth of his soul the words which all humanity will one day echo: "My Lord and my God." No other category is big enough. God! God himself! He has visited and redeemed his people.

Let me conclude with a personal testimony. The one desolating doubt I have had in my adult religious life was on this question. It was midnight in my soul, but I emerged more sure than ever, and the passing years deepen my conviction. I am quite sure now. Christ was incarnate God. He is utterly trustworthy. Travel with him, and travel with confidence. (Forgive me if I sound presumptuous, but I have tested him and been tested, in many ways.) I am in no doubt that God spoke through the Hebrew prophets and the Eastern sages, but his fullest final word was Christ. All men must come to him at the last. He has the answer to the problems of our private lives, our families, our business, our civic and national affairs. Apart from his triumph I see no hopeful prospect for our race. He is our rightful Lord and God.

I offer him to you again.

He can't rule the world till he rules you. For some of you it could be *now*, but, if it can't be now, God speed the day when you can get down beside Thomas and say, with utter sincerity, "My Lord and my God."

7

Bearing His Reproach

*Let us therefore go forth unto him without the camp,
bearing his reproach*—Heb. 13:13

DO YOU REMEMBER WHAT A SIN OFFERING WAS AS LAID DOWN IN
the Old Testament? It says in the book of Leviticus that if the
whole assembly of the people shall sin, a young bullock must be
sacrificed, and, when the blood of the bullock has been sprinkled
in the holy place, its carcass shall be carried outside the camp,
lest it pollute the place where the people lived. The Mosaic Law
called it "a sin-offering for the assembly," and a sin offering must
not remain within the camp.

Reverent students of Scripture have long seen in Jesus the con-
summation of all the ancient sacrifices of Israel, and it has been
noticed as something of minor but interesting significance that
he also suffered *without the camp.*

> There is a green hill far away,
> Without a city wall. . . .

"Without a city wall?"

That means, of course, *"outside the city wall"*—"without the
camp." *He* was the sin offering, and though the full inwardness of
what they were doing was hidden from his murderers at the

time (and is beyond our *full* understanding even yet), they bore him to a hill *outside* the city and, "He hung and suffered there.") Cast out! Despised and rejected of men! Not permitted to "pollute" the habitation of the people! And there, at the Place of the Skull, with no encircling wall to give the gallows any homeliness, he "yielded up the ghost."

So the author of this epistle says to the people of his day, "Let us therefore go forth unto him without the camp, bearing his reproach." He was writing to a suffering people, to people who had endured persecution and had still more persecution to endure, who knew what it was to be despised as followers of the Nazarene—covered with obloquy and soaked in shame. "Let us therefore go forth unto him without the camp, bearing his reproach."

Has this word significance for us today? We live in a country nominally Christian. What can this mean for us: "without the camp—bearing his reproach?" Do the words have meaning still?

I

The words *have* meaning still. Get this fact fixed firmly in your mind. *There is a reproach in this gospel*—even in a nominally Christian land. There is a shame at the heart of the cross, and it must be borne. You cannot have the hearty friendship of the world and the saving friendship of Christ. It cannot be "all this" (if "all this," you mean things which your conscience condemns) "and heaven too." There is a choice to be made, and if you are going to be definite in discipleship, it must be faced: this or that, right or wrong, God or mammon. Let me prove that to you. Let me begin to prove it in little ways.

1. *There is a social ostracism which Christians often suffer:* a sense of being shut out, not in the camp, barred from the general fellowship.

I was visiting a Christian friend of mine recently in his lovely home, and, thinking of his generosity and hospitality, I said, "I suppose all your neighbors are your friends?"

His face puckered a little, and he hesitatingly answered, "Not really. We should *like* them to be, but all their social engagements are cocktail parties. When we went and kept to soft drinks, they lost what little taste they had for our company. They seem incapable of fellowship without drink. They think you positively queer not to join them. We are really rather lonely here."

And only a week or two ago I was talking to a lovely girl I know whose life is similarly lonely in a seaside resort because her husband is an officer in the army and on perilous service overseas. When I inquired what social life she had in the neighborhood, she replied, rather sadly, "Practically none. There are plenty of other officers' wives here, but the only thing they seem to care for is bridge—morning, noon, and night—and it's always for money. Because I won't join in, they all think I'm a frump. Life is rather lonely for me. . . ."

Can you understand both of those illustrations? I think you can. There is a social ostracism that Christians of the Puritan tradition (however gay in spirit they may be) must endure.

2. There is more than that.

Sometimes a man suffers in his professional advancement because he has identified himself with the Christian cause.

I could give many better instances, but perhaps you would forgive a simple personal reminiscence.

In my army days I had great ambitions—forgive my confessing so much—to get on the educational staff of my battalion. I was an auxiliary lecturer for a long time, and I had a comfortable understanding in my own mind (and other people had too) that when a vacancy fell due, I would get it. The vacancy fell due—

and I didn't get it. I will not deny that I was inwardly grieved and wondered why.

A friend of mine, already on the staff, enlightened me. He said, "The officer in charge wouldn't have you. You finished yourself off with him that night, months and months ago, when you came and borrowed the education tent for a weekly meeting of prayer and Christian fellowship.

"You should have heard what he said when you'd gone! He's the kind of man who carries picture post cards of nude women in his pocket. He has a mind like a cesspool. I've heard him say more than once, referring to you, 'Whatever happens here, we won't have that Holy Joe on the staff.' "

3. *Sometimes Christians are actually made a joke, a butt, an object of common contumely, because they are in this way of life.* I question whether zealous Christians have been accused of anything more often than they have been accused of madness. At Pentecost the apostles were thought to be silly through drunkenness, and when Paul pleaded his case before Agrippa, Festus, the Roman Procurator, said, "Paul, thou art beside thyself; much learning doth make thee mad."

I had in my hand recently the reminiscences of Sarah Bentley, one of the lovely early evangelicals of Yorkshire, who was, indeed, at the time of her conversion, a barmaid in the George Inn at York. When the great experience came to her, everybody said, "Sally's gone daft." She said herself, "They treated me like a mad woman who mustn't be left alone."

Not all Christians, of course, are suspected of madness, and it is no compliment that the dark suspicion doesn't fall. Often it means that their lives are so tepid, so lacking in challenge, so wanting in the penetrating power of holiness and the "arrestings" of grace that they are not conspicious in society and could pass for a pagan anywhere.

But where this life is vital, this consequence often goes with it. You are put outside on the mat. You are made to feel that you don't belong to the set. You suffer mild, or not so mild, ostracism; you may endure setbacks in your calling; you may be the subject of covert sneers. You are outside the camp.

> It is the way the Master went;
> Should not the servant tread it still?

II

Now, having esetablished that, I want to hasten and say this: *Don't increase the reproach unnecessarily.*

What do I mean by that?

1. *Don't cultivate eccentricity.* There are some people who almost delight in being odd. I have known Christian men in this generation—though they are fortunately rare—who feel that the old vow of the Nazarite is obligatory today and who neither shave nor have their hair cut, regarding it as a sin to do so. You may never have met such people, but I have, and I say deliberately that the danger of that kind of oddity is this: it gives the impression to people outside that Evangelical Christians are queer. It gets them a name for being freaks when (as we know) they are among the most sweetly sane people on earth.

When Methodism first began to spread through this land, the Quaker people were already doing a fine work. John Wesley recognized that and gave God thanks for it, but the Quakers had certain oddities he couldn't approve. They wouldn't wear garments which had been dyed on the grounds that dyeing was a form of deceit. In common speech they used archaisms and addressed other people as "thee" where we would say "you," and they would say "thine" where we would say "yours." They would not use the normal names for the days of the week, Sunday, Monday, and so on, on the ground that they included pagan deities, and always said "First Day, Second Day."

I am sure John Wesley wouldn't have approved the schoolboy howler, "A Quaker is two crotchets," because he thought, as we do, so very highly of the Society of Friends, but John Wesley did make this rule for his people: "We do not place our religion, or any part of it, in being attached to any peculiar mode of speaking, any quaint or uncommon set of expressions. . . ."

That rule still runs. Don't be eccentric in speech. Said Wesley (in effect), "When you quote the Scripture, quote them in their own words, but, apart from that, do not deviate from the most usual way of speaking."

I know Christians who never use their vote, not because, on one particular occasion, they were so confused on the issue that they didn't know what to do, but on every occasion and on principle because they say that they mean to keep themselves "unspotted from the world." If, therefore, a saint and a demon were rival candidates at an election (which pre-election publicity sometimes suggests!), these people would still not vote, contracting out, as it were, from the issues of our social life.

Avoid, I beg you, eccentricities. Don't cultivate peculiarities. Christ came to save and sanctify our humanity—not to make us quaint and queer.

2. In the second place, don't be censorious. A great deal of harm has been done in the world by the censoriousness of the good. You may have made a rule for yourself never to go to a place of entertainment. All right! You are at perfect liberty to abstain, but don't cast aspersions on people who enjoy a good film now and then. You may be a nonsmoker. I am myself. I bought my library out of the tobacco I never smoked, and I think my health has been better for my abstention. But you can be a nonsmoker without being an anti-smoker. It isn't proved

that a pipe a day is a sin. If God wants a man to give up tobacco altogether, leave the Lord or the doctor to tell him so. Personal evangelism is not well begun by taking a man, as it were, by the lapel of his coat and saying, "No pint, no pipe, and no pools." If he comes into the fellowship of Christian people, he will learn why some Christians object to all three, but if you get a reputation for being a crank, people won't heed you when you are dealing with the most grave moral issues. When you speak out against adultery, they will say to one another: "You can't take any notice of *him!* He wouldn't let a man smoke a pipe if he could prevent it." Be quietly firm in your own way of living but only use the word "sin" as the New Testament uses it. There are too many real sins in the world without our inventing any.

Censoriousness is a wretched sin. The admixture of pride in it explains that. If there is a thing all men seem to resent it is that "holier than thou" manner, and it has done more harm to good religion than many other more obvious sins.

3. In the third place settle with yourself that, as a Christian, *you will never sever fellowship with other people if you can avoid it.*

Imagine a young fellow, a member of a set of gay sparks whose whole idea of life in their twenties is to enjoy themselves, and this young man is arrested by the Holy Spirit and drawn by God into his way of life. Some Christians would tell him to sever his fellowship with his old friends at once. "Forsake them," they would say. "Cut them off! Finish with them!" I say quite the contrary: "Don't forsake them. Hold on to Christ first, but hold on to them too. You may be God's supreme opportunity in their life. If the fellowship is to end, let *them* break it." If your fellowship with them became a peril to your soul, God would warn you and tell you what to do, but if Christians are always going to withdraw themselves from the world, where will it get us? There is a great deal of good in plain, ordinary people. There is, indeed, a divine spark in them, and God might use you to fan it to a flame. We shall be living little segregated lives, with less and less influence on the modern world, if we are continually "withdrawing" from all these social contacts. If we believe in individual salvation but have no interest in society, we shall be like men arriving at a great fire, willing to rescue a person here and there from the holocaust but quite unwilling to assist the authorities in putting out the blaze.

III

But what happens if, having avoided censoriousness and eccentricity and remained, God helping us, sweetly human—*what happens if they still exclude us from the camp*, still thrust us out and treat us almost as if were pariahs?

Ah! *What then?*

Being sure that you are not a foolish eccentric, and not proudly censorious and not yourselves quitting the fellowship, but being thrust out, *exult in it!*

Say to yourself, "This is not *my* reproach. It is *his!* This is the shame of Jesus—crucified stark naked on a cross—and I am allowed to bear a bit of his shame. Hallelujah!"

Why is it that this reproach centers so often in the name of Jesus?

A fine Christian woman I know, who bears a witness for our Lord in an unsavory factory, brought that very problem to me some time ago. She said, "I can talk to the girls I work with about religion now and then, about moral standards, even about God, and they take it in silence, if not in acquiescence. But if I talk about Jesus, they will *not* take it; they seem to find his name offensive."

I knew what she meant.

Do you?

Jesus is the Name we treasure,
  Name beyond what words can tell;
Name of gladness, Name of pleasure,
  Ear and heart delighting well;
Name of sweetness passing measure,
  Saving us from sin and hell.

But it is a name others find offensive. They turn it into a swear word, a blasphemous oath. It is one of the bitterest experiences a Christian must endure to hear that holy name profanely used.

When that tide of reproach is rolling over you, when, for Christ's sake, you are made an object of reviling, "rejoice and be exceeding glad, for great is your reward in heaven; for so persecuted they the prophets which were before you."

In the late seventies of the last century there was a girl named Priscilla Livingstone Stewart. She was lovely to look upon: blue eyes, bright-colored golden hair, Irish gaiety. All the boys in the neighborhood thought she was grand. Her admirers lined up for a smile!

Then she met Christ. Having been heartily opposed to religion before, she became as ardent a disciple, and, soon after, the Salvation Army came to those parts. It was altogether characteristic of her that she could throw in her lot for a while with that despised people, and she chose to walk in their procession in days when they were pelted with old boots, stones, bad oranges, and worse eggs. Now, notice this! I give you the exact words of her reminiscences. She said, "None of my friends recognized me in the street, and all the young men who were fond of me walked on the other side."

I have no doubt that, being a normal girl, there was something of pain for her in that, but she felt that she had gained infinitely more than she had lost, and, truth to tell, God had other things in store for her. She went as a missionary to China and became the wife of that extraordinary missionary, C. T. Studd.

"None of my friends recognized me now"—"without the camp"—"bearing his reproach." What do you do when, without eccentricity and censoriousness and with no willing severance of old friendships on your part, they put you out?

You exult in it!

Don't miss the willing eagerness of the first phrase in my text: "Let us therefore go forth unto him. . . ." I am not going to be dragged. I am going willingly. Indeed, I am running. It is an honor of which I am all unworthy. I am going to thrust my shoulder underneath his cross and bear whatever I can of his reproach.

> I'm not ashamed to own my Lord,
> Or to defend His cause,
> Maintain the honour of His word,
> The glory of His Cross.

8

God's Law Is Not "On Approval"

The law of Jehovah is perfect,
restoring the soul—Ps. 19:7

A CURIOUS THING HAPPENED IN THE COURTS THE OTHER DAY. A MAN was charged with having a shortwave radio set and not possessing a license. He pleaded an unusual defense. He said that the set was not really his, that he had received it from a dealer only "on approval," and until he decided to buy it, he didn't feel under obligation to take out a license. He could not agree that he was breaking the law.

The judge fined him. "The law knows nothing about 'approval,'" he said. "The law is to be obeyed. Pay the fine!"

Will you notice that, please? It is more important than it seems on the surface: "The law knows nothing about approval. The law is to be obeyed."

Many people talk today as though the contrary were true. One falls in with people who say, "I don't profess to be religious." They ignore divine worship. They live as though God were not there. Some of them have no respect for moral prohibitions, and, if you display the slightest surprise at their conduct, they fling this defense in your teeth. They say, as though nothing more need be said, "I don't profess to be religious."

Now, let us look at the theory which lies behind this statement. It would seem, in the minds of many people, that the law is only binding upon you if you approve of it. It appears that the unexpressed reasoning is this: "If you don't approve the law, it has no power to bind you. If you don't recognize the rule, you cannot be held by its demands. If you reject the law, because it is too hard or not to your taste, it ceases to exercise authority." They say, in effect, "The law does not apply to me. I considered it once 'on approval,' and I didn't approve!"

And that is the world we are living in at the present time. Not only the moral teaching of the Sermon on the Mount, but the Ten Commandments are mocked with impunity by millions of people. Even in our one-time-honest land, pilfering is common. The institution of marriage is breaking down. Our prisons are overcrowded.

Nor does there seem to be any widespread remorse at the sin of it. When these bare-faced delinquents are found out, they often feel no shame.

However did men and women come to think so lightly of the majesty of the moral law? By what specious self-deception did they convince themselves that the rules of God could be ignored? Is it possible to pierce their minds and see how this tragic error came about?

I think it is.

It is well known to all students both of ethics and of law that there are half-a-dozen ways of using the word "law" which are really quite distinct. A law of nature is quite a different thing from a law of association. A law of England may be altogether distinct from a law of God. There are laws which can be changed and laws which can't. There are laws which can be violated and others quite inviolable. It is a pity we have to use the same word to describe these different concepts, for there is little doubt that in this confusion of meanings, many people have been trapped into sin.

I

Notice, first, that there are *some laws* which *apply only to the people who accept them*. I mean, of course, the laws of voluntary associations.

These laws are made by little groups of people who associate themselves together in order to pursue within the community some particular aim. It may be a debating society or a community choir. The association is entirely voluntary. No one is compelled to join, and the simple basis in each case is clear and defined: to debate or to sing the works of the great composers.

Now, these societies have their own laws and rules, and if anybody doesn't like them, he can leave. No harm has been done. The law is only intended to apply to those who want it to apply to them. A member of the debating society may object to the rule that no man, speaking from the floor, may speak for more than three minutes. He may feel that the golden thoughts which surge from his mind can never be telescoped into so short a time, and that other people should sit and listen while he talks as long as he likes. Being convinced about that, he simply leaves, and when he leaves, the laws of the society no longer apply to him.

A member of the choir may object that he or she is never selected for solo parts and, being bound by the rule that the musical director decides these things, withdraws from membership.

Now, all that is perfectly clear. Where it concerns voluntary associations, the law only applies to those who desire that it apply to them.

But who seriously suggests that the human race is a voluntary association? We are born, without our choice, in a way our Maker devised, into a family life he planned, and under conditions which he laid down.

Moreover, it is virtually impossible for any individual to withdraw from human association. The hermit tried to do so, but he was still dependent on the alms and gifts of other people who gave freely from the fruit of their toil. Even if a man *could* withdraw from all human society, he has still not withdrawn from the rule and authority of God.

Even when you were a prodigal—if you ever were a prodigal—and made your home in the far country and dined at the swine troughs, even there you did not cease to be a subject of his rule. You were estranged, antagonistic, seeking to live as though you did not belong, but you were never outside the compass of his law. God's laws apply to all men, and his moral demands press on them, whether they regard themselves as being his subjects or not. You cannot cancel out the imperative demands of the Ten Commandments by snapping your fingers and saying, "I don't profess to be religious."

God never promulgated his law for human approval. He promulgated it for human obedience. The Scriptures never suggest that you can take it or leave it. The Scriptures say:

The law of Jehovah is perfect, restoring the soul:
The testimony of Jehovah is sure, making wise the simple.
The precepts of Jehovah are right, rejoicing the heart:
The commandment of Jehovah is pure, enlightening the eyes.
The fear of Jehovah is clean, enduring for ever:
The ordinances of Jehovah are true, and righteous altogether.

If you are thinking about buying a garment, you can take it or leave it. If you are thinking about buying a house, you can take it or leave it. If you are thinking about buying a car, you can take it or leave it.

But when you are thinking about the law of God, you can only take it. If you break it, ultimately it will break you.

G. K. Chesterton said that there was once a man who disbelieved in the law of gravity, and to prove his disbelief, he walked off the edge of a cliff. He did not prove his disbelief. He proved the law of gravity.

The moral law of God is not the same as a law of nature. The laws of nature are both unchangeable and inviolable, while the moral laws of God, though unchangeable, are not, of course, inviolable. You can break them. That is the tragedy of our world. Millions do!

But they cannot be broken with impunity. Sooner or later they will break you. Where his moral laws are disregarded, the bill is bound to come in. He has made a world which will only work his way. When the consequences of wrongdoing come down upon us, we raise piteous protests to heaven, but it is no use saying, "I didn't profess to believe." For our own good the law works on independently of our unimportant opinions, and what a man sows, that shall he also reap.

What do you suppose would happen in a human court if a prisoner, charged with assault and battery, told the judge that he didn't profess to be good? His effrontery would only stiffen the sentence because he had added impertinence to assault and battery.

I say it again: Morality is not a thing for approval. It is not to be thought of in terms of the laws of voluntary associations. It is binding upon all of us, and none is outside its sway.

II

A second reason why people have come to disregard the moral law turns upon the fact that *some laws do vary with localities*—national laws, for instance!

It is a crime in parts of Switzerland to cut down your own tree without planting two others; it is not a crime in England. It is a crime in England to run a gaming house; it is not a crime in many countries on the continent. It is a crime in Turkey to wear a fez (or it was when I was there); it is not a crime in Egypt.

Laws like these vary with localities and alter at frontiers. Consequently, some people suppose that law is not an austere and static canon but something conventional, founded on the changing whim and will of the people, and no more to be solemnly regarded than the thousand other customs with which contemporary life is hedged about.

That, indeed, is how the Greeks felt when they first went to Egypt. Few things (so students of ancient history tell us) make more diverting reading than the stories of the first Greeks who visited the great empire of the Nile. They had never guessed there was so strange a land in all the world. Everything seemed upside down.

They were used enough to lizards in Greece, but in Egypt lizards grew to the size of nightmares, and, moreover, they were real! Crocodiles were new to the Greeks.

The great river of Egypt reversed all the obvious laws of nature. Greek rivers were torrents in winter but dried up in the summer. Summer was the season when the Nile was at the full and overflowed its banks.

To the Grecian mind the people of Egypt did everything the wrong way around.

In Egypt the women went to market to buy and sell, while the men remained at home to weave.

What the Greeks did indoors, the Egyptians did outdoors, and vice versa.

The Greeks almost gave it up. All the laws and customs of the Greeks seemed reversed in Egypt, and the Greek was tempted to believe, therefore, that laws varied with locality. Men have been tempted to believe that dangerous error ever since.

Let us be clear about this. Whatever may be true of the laws and customs of nations, the law of the Lord does not vary with locality. God does not ask one thing of an Englishman and another of a German and a third of a Japanese.

The law of the Lord is perfect; the testimony of the Lord is sure; the precepts of the Lord are right. And they are perfect, sure, and right the whole world over. Their perfection consists in their being *just* calculated for our spiritual growth. Man-made rules and regulations may and, indeed, *do* vary with localities, and we can see why in some senses, it should be so.

But we cannot lift that human contrivance to the heavens and affirm such vacillations of our God. His law applies whether we like it or not, and his law applies everywhere: among the Pygmies and the Eskimos, at the Equator and in Antarctica, in the palace and in the cottage too.

When America was "dry," many Americans living on the Canadian border made a practice of walking into Canada to get a drink. They felt that that was better than surreptitious drinking. Prohibition didn't apply in Canada. You could drink there and still respect the law.

But there is no national barrier you can cross and legitimately flout the law of God. It knows no frontiers. It is for *all* men— everywhere.

III

The final misconception about law that trips people into disregard of the law of God is the fact that *some laws alter with passing time.*

Again, I may instance the laws of nations.

That which is law in one age is not necessarily law in another.

Contrast, for instance, the penal law of this age with the penal law in England at the time of Wesley. Do you know that there were no less than 160 different crimes for which men, women, and children in England could be hanged when Wesley first began his apostolic ministry? There are only two today.

In those days, in England, you could be hanged if you picked a pocket for more than a shilling, if you grabbed goods from someone's hands and ran away with them, if you took from a store wares valued at more than five shillings, if you stole a horse or a sheep or even ensnared a rabbit on a gentleman's estate. Charles Wesley records in one place in his journal that he was preaching in a prison to fifty-two felons who were waiting to be hanged—and one of them was a little boy of ten!

Think how the law has altered in less than two hundred years. It seems, indeed, to be another world.

Or look at it this way. Think of all the remedial work which has been done by the Factory Acts in still more recent days. I had need, years ago, to look into the labor conditions which were operative in a certain chrome factory in southern Scotland at the end of the last century. I found the workers were paid three pence to four pence an hour, that they worked a twelve-hour day, with no time off for meals, that many of them worked a seven-day week, and that the whole industrial process in which they were engaged was most dangerous to their health.

Think how the laws have changed since then!

Consequently, people say that law is subject to change and needs constant revision—and then they slide foolishly in their thinking from those man-made regulations to the solemn moral laws of God.

The laws of God have been the same in every age. The Factory Acts may require revision but not the Ten Commandments. They are eternal, written in the heavens, and binding on all generations. Every age makes its efforts to subvert them, and our own age has been no exception. Indeed, our own generation has witnessed, in some directions, as serious and evil an attack upon the ethics of the New Testament as has been known for centuries. But those efforts cannot affect the sublime truth.

Sometimes, when one reads the newspapers, one is left with the impression that it is a more heinous sin in certain social circles to break one rule of etiquette than to disregard the whole Ten Commandments. But still the law stands and has its own way of vindicating itself. Men seem to break it, but, in the end, it breaks them.

The fear of the Lord is clean, enduring for ever.

I was reading a while ago of the early history of white settlements in South Africa, and I came across some strange eccentric characters.

One of them was called Ikey Sonnenberg. Ikey ran a store catering to the needs of the Boers, many of whom were simple and pious men whom Ikey did not find it hard to deceive.

One day a Boer was selling his wool to Ikey. The woolbales were weighed, and the price was fixed at three pence per pound. Ikey made a rapid calculation and announced that the total amounted to 153 pounds.

The farmer consulted his ready-reckoner and said, "No, according to my reckoner the total is 173 pounds. Whereupon Ikey seized the Boer's ready reckoner, rapidly examined it, and exclaimed, "Good heavens, you're using last year's ready reckoner. It's worthless *this* year."

The old Boer meekly received the correction and was content to accept the amount that Ikey was eager to pay.

Ikey caught the Boer. He wouldn't have caught you. You would have said that a ready reckoner does not vary from year to year. You would have said that what is true in mathematics now will be true in mathematics tomorrow.

And with greater confidence you may say, "What is true in the law of God now, and what was true in the moral law of God in the dim dawn of Bible history will be true in the law of God for all the generations which may succeed us."

Our apprehensions of his will may vary; our obedience most certainly does. But *the law of the Lord does not change.*

In the midst, therefore, of an age which flouts that holy law, which suggests that it can be taken on approval, or rejected, according to taste, which blasphemously supposes that his law can be affected by locality and altered by time, we stand foursquare in opposition and call that talk "dangerous and deceptive nonsense." We say again, "The law of the Lord is perfect, restoring the soul."

9

The Pacemakers

They that receive abundance of grace—Rom. 5:17

I

WE DO NOT ALL TRAVEL ALONG THE ROAD OF CHRISTIAN DIS-cipleship at the same rate. We get old at the same rate! However different the feelings may be, a year is as long for a lad in his teens as for a man in his seventies, but progress in Christian discipleship is not made at a fixed rate. Some people grow more rapidly in five years than others grow in fifty. Some people have been on the Christian pathway nearly all their life, but they move at a snail's pace, while others cover twice the distance in ten years.

Think of C. T. Studd, the astonishing missionary. When he had his deep religious experience, he was thinking of being a lawyer. Within a month he gave up his plans for a legal career, offered himself for immediate missionary work in China, only lingered long enough in England to address a series of meetings and to tell people why he was going, and then, straight to the heart of China to share with others the great secret which he had found.

Two years after he arrived in China, he attained his twenty-fifth birthday and inherited 29,000 pounds from his father. In a week or two he had given it away. I am not sure that he would have said that everybody who inherited a fortune should give it away. But he felt that *he* must! He feared (like John Wesley) that money might make "a home in his heart."

What a pacemaker! What an "out-and-outer"! He was a veteran in five years. Few people could stay the peace set by C. T. Studd.

Contrast that with the thousands of people who claim to be in this way of life—and are in this way of life in some degree—but who, after thirty years of discipleship, are still peevish, petty, mean, gossipy, selfish and fall to the same sins which so easily trapped them before they had any personal encounter with Christ at all.

I remember a day I once spent in County Durham with a friend of mine—a coal miner. He is a man in middle life now. Before his conversion he was a drunken sot. He was a cheat as well. Playing once in a dominoes competition, he covered a dot with a bit of chewing gum and cleared the "kitty" of twenty-nine pounds.

He had a good mother and a good wife, and he came near to breaking the heart of both of them. One day his mother said to his wife, "Leave him, Nellie. Leave him! He'll drag you to hell!"

But Nellie didn't leave him, nor ceased to pray, and one wonderful Sunday evening she had the answer to her prayers. Spent up and miserably sober, he yielded to her pleading and went with her to evening worship where a friend of mine was preaching his characteristically powerful evangelical word. When, at the end of the sermon, my friend made an appeal, Jack stumbled forward and asked God to forgive him.

What an hour! I think he only ever glanced back once—and it was but a glance! He was transformed in the astonished gaze of all the neighborhood. In the passing of only a few years, the

Holy Spirit wiped from his face all the marks of dissipation and made him radiant with an unearthly light.

When I first knew him, I had been ordained twice as long as he had been converted, and there are some things I can do, I suppose, that he can't do. But, oh, there are many more important things that *he* can do which I can't do. It is wonderful to hear him talk to men who have missed their way—such love, such incisiveness, such skill with sinners. I know he has traveled the road of Christian discipleship faster than I have done.

II

Now, why is this? Why do some people travel faster? You have felt it yourself, haven't you? Surely you have met people younger than you are in discipleship and yet able to forgive injuries done to them, gloriously free of that nasty censoriousness that sometimes afflicts you, untainted by jealousy, glad to see others doing more effectively the things they want to do themselves and praising them for it. All this you have noticed in people who were wallowing in sin long after you had been drawn to our way of life, and now they have sped past you because, maybe, you are mean and petty still!

Why?

The answer, quite simply, is this. They have received an "abundance of grace." They have noted my text "Abundance of Grace," and with eager longing they have opened themselves to it.

What do we mean by grace?

Grace has been variously defined and does not mean precisely the same in the Old Testament as in the New (though the meanings are related). Let me mention some of the flavors of meaning in this most important word.

It meant favor and kindness and (strangely perhaps) the gratitude, also, which the favor evoked. Its central meaning in the New Testament is of God's undeserved mercy in redeeming mankind.

"Grace" as an undeserved favor is still used in business. The insurance company uses it sometimes when they say, concerning an appeal, "Well, in these circumstances you have no *claim*, but we will give you something *as an act of grace!* They acknowledge no indebtedness, but out of their kindness (and in hope of business to come!) they give you something to which you have no right.

I suppose it was inevitable in Christian usage that the word "grace" should come to mean, also, not only the unmerited loving kindness of God, but almost the power he lent to mortals for their sanctification too.

These people who speed past us on the path of Christian discipleship have received more of that power which God imparts "unmerited and free," and by which they are able to overleap all the impediments of their onward way.

"But *why* have they received more grace?" you ask. "*Why?*" If it is by favor, does that mean that God has favorites? Is there anything capricious in the help of the Almighty? Is God like some men we have met, biased in his affections, with some inexplicable preference for one person and lack of preference for another? Surely God does not take what we call "a fancy" to some people and not to others?

Oh, no! There is no favoritism of that kind on God's part. He shows favor, true, but it is what the world's greatest hymn writer calls an "undistinguishing regard." His favors move to all.

And if you still ask me, "Then *why* have these people received more grace than I have received?" I will tell you. Let me see if I can make it plain.

III

First, they knew that this grace was there to be had. They had dwelt on this and similar texts: an "abundance of grace."

They didn't think that God's dealings with them were over when they first surrendered to him. Some Christians do. They seem to feel that God's only concern is to get us on the pilgrim way. You can tell this from their conversation. Their religious talk is only of their conversion. They seem totally unaware that God's supreme concern is not to call them "saints," but *make* them saints, not just to cancel the sin but break its power in them, not merely to *impute* righteousness but to *impart* it also.

But not these pacemakers we are considering now! They see their committal, not as a completion but as a commencement, not as something rounded-off but as something just begun.

God has more to give! Of that they are sure, and they keep it in mind all the time. It saves them from self-complacency. Always there is a sense of expectation in them. "There is more to have!"

2. Not only did they remember that there was more grace to have, but they wanted it *ardently*. They wanted it more than anything else. It seemed to them to be a treasure above all treasures. They had valued the values of earth, and they had said to themselves, "Nothing is so precious as grace."

You may have heard the name Fletcher of Madeley, that great friend of John Wesley, the man whom Wesley designated as his successor in the leadership of the Methodist people, though, (as it happened), Fletcher died before John Wesley and never came to the succession. Fletcher's biographer says of him: "He was more than Christian; he was Christlike." Wesley said he was the finest man he had ever met. When he had the solemn duty of preaching Fletcher's funeral sermon, he took a text from the Psalms: "Mark the perfect man."

Fletcher once made an important public utterance on a question which was agitating the country at the time and rendered a signal service to the government of the day. He didn't do it for that reason. He was—as ever—speaking what he believed to be true, but it had that consequence, and the ministers of the crown noticed it. Fletcher was not only a Methodist preacher but, like John Wesley, a clergyman of the established church as well, and it occurred to the Lord Chancellor that in return for this service Fletcher had rendered some preferment should be offered him, "some promotion," as plain people would say. That kind of thing is possible in a state church—and there was a time when it was done.

When the official despatched by the Lord Chancellor called on the seraphic Fletcher at Madeley, he was at some pains delicately to hint at his errand, but the holy man was slow to take the hint. (Saints are terribly dull in some ways. Their wits are not sharpened by self-interest.) Finally, to make himself clear, the visitor asked if there was anything Mr. Fletcher wanted? The government would be very happy to . . . if . . . Mr. Fletcher would understand . . .

And then perhaps some understanding *did* break on the mind of that good man, and he said, "How kind! How very kind! But I want nothing . . . *except more grace.*"

He only wanted more grace! I wonder what the visitor made of that. I wonder what report he gave to the Lord Chancellor. "He doesn't want anything. There is nothing you have that attracts him. He only wants more grace!"

That is one test of the saints. They have looked at the values of earth in the light of heaven. They have seen the folly of accumulating riches, the absurdity of heaping together the treasures of earth, the meaninglessness of angling for titles. They know that the only really valuable thing is grace. "Let me have that," they say, "and I am content."

3. And now notice this. They knew that the grace was to be had. They wanted it ardently. They received it; grace for grace.

Do you remember that vibrant verse in the first chapter of John's Gospel: "For of his fullness we all received, and grace for grace"? That used to puzzle me when I was a youth. It puzzled me in my early ministry too. I wanted to preach on it, but I couldn't grasp its central meaning—and it is always an impediment in expounding a text if you don't understand it yourself!

Grace for grace? It almost suggests an exchange. How could I barter with the Almighty and not merely receive grace but offer it too? Whatever did it mean?

I think I know now. I believe that it means grace *succeeding* grace, and that our capacity to receive grace at any level depends on our use of it at a lower one. Refuse God's offer of grace at this level of your spiritual life and you have incapacitated yourself from receiving it at the next. Your reception of it here measures your ability to take it there. It isn't divine unwillingness which explains your lack of grace at this level. Your refusal of it there makes you unable to employ it on the higher plane. The progress is a step at a time, and we can't cut out the intermediate steps. We must use the present proffered grace to be able to use the grace which succeeds it.

This point isn't easy! How can I put it in a picture for you? I wonder if this will help?

I remember when I sat for my first scholarship. On the eve of the examination I was rather worried, worried about some things which didn't matter at all. I recall going to my professor and saying, "Sir, they tell me that when I get into the examination hall tomorrow, I shall find my desk by a number, and that there will be half-a-dozen sheets of paper on the desk. What will I do, sir, when I have used the paper up?"

He laughed. "You needn't worry about that," he said. "You can worry about your mathematics but not about that! At the end of the hall a gentleman in an academic gown will be sitting on a dais. He is the invigilator. If you use up your paper, just go and ask him for more."

"Can I?" I said, much relieved. "Will he give me all I want?"

He laughed again. "All you can use!" he said.

It turned out just as he told me. When my racing pen had covered the paper (pent-up with an eagerness you younger people may not know in these days when the road to the university is much less impeded for people of limited means than it was then), I ran down the aisle between the desks and panted to the invigilator, "Paper! Paper!"

He just gave it to me. All I could use.

God is so eager to give his grace—and there is so much of it.

> Grace is flowing like a river
> Millions there have been supplied . . .

but it can't be wasted! You can have all you can use, but to have more you must use what you have.

To put it still plainer—and to linger a moment longer in the academic world—you *graduate* in its use. A man can't walk into a university and submit himself for a doctorate. He must be a master first in his field of study.

He can't walk in and just submit himself for examination as a master. He must be a bachelor first and (in the university I know best) an honors bachelor too. So it runs. There is nothing foolish and arbitrary about it. Superficial slickness isn't scholarship. It is only as you absorb learning at one level that you are able to absorb it at another. We advance. We *graduate*. So it is with grace. With infinite patience God is leading us on, but we can't cut out any step he knows to be necessary. That is what some of you have tried to do. This is the reason why—having begun the life of discipleship with zest—you've slackened off and move so slowly now that it is almost a question whether you are moving at all.

Do you remember the disappointment Paul felt over some of the Galatians? He said to them in his letter: "Ye *did* run well." "Ye *did!*"

Might the Saviour say as much to you? How keen you were once! It wasn't just your youth. You were responding to grace, and it came in like the waves of the sea—grace succeeding grace.

This is what I suspect. The time came when God led you to some new task or surrender—of time, talents, money, service— and you sheered off. God never proffers a task without proffering the grace it requires, and, in refusing the task, you refused the grace. That's when you ran on the sandbank. People who started long after you have swept past you. You try to conceal the truth perhaps from yourself and put your lack of keenness down to your age, but you are unconvincing. God needs the whole of you, as much now as he ever did. What are you going to do if my words carry conviction to your mind?

This is what I suggest.

Before you sleep tonight, get alone and be quiet with God. Let there be no breathlessness about you. Have all the time it takes.

Review your life in God's light. Where did you fall out of the race? Was it here . . . or here . . . or here? You may find the very place. Even if you don't, the time will not be wasted. God never refuses his grace to us, and he meets us *just where we are*.

Tell him that you want to be back in things again, pacing forward spiritually with the most ardent souls you know.

It will make the angels sing in heaven. "Look!" they will say. "He's moving once more. He's moving with speed. He'll be a pacemaker again!"

10

Three Groans

The whole creation groaneth. . .—Rom. 8:22
We ourselves groan within ourselves. . .—Rom. 8:23
The Spirit himself maketh intercession for us with groanings which cannot be uttered—Rom. 8:26

A MINISTER WAS TELLING ME A WHILE AGO THAT HE WAS CALLED to the bedside of a dying man. When he arrived at the house, the man's wife said, "I'm afraid there isn't any purpose now in your coming. He has lapsed into unconsciousness, and I don't think he'll come around again." The minister said, "Nevertheless, I will pray beside him." As the family gathered around the bed, he prayed, and, as he concluded his prayer, the dying man (from some deep level of his unconsciousness), to the astonishment of them all, said quite clearly, "Amen." Then he groaned three times and died.

Three groans! Let me use that scrap of pastoral experience as a mere device for diving into a consideration of the three groans of Paul.

Paul mentioned three groans in swift succession:

1. The whole creation *groaneth.* . . .
2. We ourselves *groan* within ourselves. . . .
3. The Spirit himself maketh intercession for us with *groanings* which cannot be uttered.

I want us—for spiritual purposes which will be plain as I proceed —to listen to those three groans.

I

First then—"*the whole creation groaneth.*"

Who can doubt it? Hungary, Poland, Suez, Cyprus, South Africa, Malaya—the whole creation groaneth. At any moment of time, when we look at the organized life of men, we see distress somewhere and hear the groans of unhappy people. Nor is it only abroad. Open your newspaper almost any day and read the headlines of the home news—murders, robberies, rape, divorce, juvenile delinquency, overcrowded prisons.

Nor is the groan *in human* nature only. Everything that lives is subject to disease: animals, birds, fish, flowers, trees, plants. Life seems strangely poisoned near the fount.

Years ago, traveling in Egypt, I saw my first water buffalo. He was having his daily soak. A man standing by noticed my interest and said that the water buffalo was the only living creature not subject to disease, and when I got home, I quoted this remark to a zoologist. He denied it at once. He said that the water buffalo was a hardy beast, but along with everything else that lives, it was subject to disease. Everything living is tainted. The whole creation groaneth. That is why some people find it so hard to believe in the love of God. It isn't easy to connect the diseases and warrings of animals with human sin.

The lady who wrote the hymn we teach our children—"All Things Bright and Beautiful"—was only looking at *some* of the things which she might have noticed, the things which were "bright and beautiful." She mentions, it is true, "the cold wind in the winter," but there is no verse about the tiger or the snake. You get the idea? It wasn't *all* creation she had in view. She was being selective. She wasn't seeing nature "whole." But Paul did!

When he looked at creation, he looked at all of it and held his faith in the face of awful problems. It was a close observer and honest man who said: "The whole creation groaneth."

There are some groans you can trace to human sin but not all of them, not the snake or the tiger or the flood. They seem to belong to the structure of creation itself and almost look like a leer on the face of the Almighty. There are some people who say that we must never be pessimists—not even if we live with optimists. It is only a week or two ago since a happy, healthy girl, soon to be married, said to me, "I think if only people would look at the world the right way, everything in it is beautiful." I said, "I am glad you think so, and I am so happy for you. . . . But don't be too hard," I added, "if some of us take a somber view of things. Only this week I have heard of the death of two friends, both in pain and neither old. Only this week I have had a letter from a young minister who is going blind before he is thirty."

Paul was right: "The whole creation groaneth. . . ."

II

Secondly, *"we ourselves groan within ourselves."*

You will doubt if that is true. "Is not *joy* the heritage of the Christian?" you will say. "Is it not the second fruit of the Spirit?"

But to have joy and inward groans is the tension in which the Christian daily lives; joy at *this* personal salvation groans at a world adrift from God. If it was only joy, how strange it would be! How can a Christian be indifferent to the fact that half of the world is hungry and a third of it is starving. How much of the mind of Christ can be in him if he can go blissfully on indifferent and half deaf to the groans of suffering humanity? If you deny that you "groan within yourself," you cannot share the compassion of Christ.

In the middle years of the last century there was a sharp controversy between the philosophers and the theologians of the Western world over man's perfectability. The philosophers were saying that man *must* become perfect, perfect on his own. They thought there was some kind of ethical evolution at work in our race, unrelated to any particular religion. "Man must become perfect," Herbert Spencer said.

The theologians (who were having the worst of the argument then) were quoting the Scriptures and saying that man was "carnal, sold under sin." That was nearly a hundred years ago, and now most people are willing to concede that the theologians were right. There is no escalator to perfection. There is no *mechanical* progress. In this century we have had two world wars and live in the shadow of a third. Man by himself cannot become perfect. Some of the philosophers themselves are saying now that, maybe, the theologians were right!

Man is carnal, sold under sin. Is it any wonder that when we think on our own sins and follies, "we ourselves groan within ourselves"?

We look back over history and see that every discovery of science has been twisted to Satanic use. Man made the airplane. What a wonderful discovery! Fancy being able to carry so swiftly the specialist in one country to the patient in another. We used it to carry bombs!

Man discovered radio and, in Britain, we formed the B.B.C., saying, "Nation shall speak peace unto nation." Now the radio is used to spout biased propaganda all over the world!

We split the atom, and the first use we made of it was a bigger and a "better" bomb!

If we turn our eyes from the world to the church, hoping to find comfort there, we shall be disappointed again. In Britain, at least, we have been falling back for years. You may say, "We are not falling back *abroad*. We are advancing on the mission field!"

Advancing? We may make 100,000 converts in a year, but, in that same year, several million more little pagans are born. We are not advancing *on the birthrate*; we are going back.

Nor is there any comfort in self-contemplation. We look at ourselves, and, if we have seen ourselves in the white light of God, we know what muddied creatures we are. We wonder if we *ever* did *anything* at *any time* for the pure love of God. Did you? Could you put your hand on your heart and say, "This I did for the love of God alone"?

So, whether we look at the groaning creation, at suffering humanity, at the half-impotent Church, or at our soiled selves, we see again that the apostle was right, and with the most solid grounds we can say, "We ourselves groan within ourselves."

III

The third text is *"The Spirit himself maketh intercession for us with groanings which cannot be uttered"*—and this is the most astonishing word of all.

The Spirit groans? A groan in the heart of God?

Oh, the bliss, the wonder, of this final word! *There is a groan in the heart of God.* Go and look at the cross whenever you are low, and see him on the wood dying to redeem you. That is the God you are dealing with! He is yearning over us all the time, longing, loving, dying for us, and symbolizing in his cross his groan for his wayward world. At the center of the universe there is a loving God like that.

I have sometimes said to people, "What is the most awful thing you can think of?" After they have thought a little, some have said, "The thought of my own death is a very somber and awful thing."

Come, now! That isn't *very* serious. Everybody has got to die, and heaven is not a bad place to go to. *That* is not the most awful thing.

Some have said that the most awful thing to them is the thought that they might permanently lose their reason. This is a solemn thing, no doubt, but you would step forward into full understanding the moment after death.

Some have said, "A third world war. That would be the worst of all!"

That certainly would be a terrible thing, but I can think of something more awful than that. *This*, in my view, is the most awful thing any human mind can conceive. Atheism! Just sheer atheism! The belief that there is nothing to believe in. That behind this universe there is *not* the loving Father whom Jesus revealed but some blind force or some big idiotic face to whom we mean nothing, that there is no sense in things, no meaning in the universe, no loving heart behind it all. That would be the most awful thing anybody could ever think of—that we do not matter, that we wink out, at the last, like a candle, that all our life ends in a handful of grey ashes. *That* is the most awful thing, *and it is not true,* for behind this universe is a God who cares so much that he groans in his love for us and yearns to redeem, that all the agencies of heaven are moving to our help, that love burns at the heart of all things. "The Spirit himself maketh intercession for us with groanings which cannot be uttered."

Notice this. All true progress in this world is by the echo of the groan of God in the heart of man. We saw a moment ago how stupid the people were who thought that there was some mechanical progress in this world, an ethical evolution independent of God, an escalator to perfection. There is no solid reason for believing that to be true.

What, then, is the hope of progress in this mundane world?

This! That the groan of God shall echo in the heart of men and women! All true progress comes that way.

How were the slaves freed in the British Empire? Did all England wake up one morning and say, "This is wrong. We must free the slaves." No! One man woke up one morning with the groan of God in his soul, and William Wilberforce and his friends labored until the most splendid hour in our history when Britain was worthy of herself, and, under no pressure from anybody but the pressure of her own conscience, paid a larger sum than her national debt to free the slaves.

How was all the social trouble after the industrial revolution ameliorated? God groaned in the head of Lord Shaftesbury, and he toiled and toiled to serve and save the poor. Progress is *not* mechanical. There is no ethical evolution in man alone. Progress is by the echo of the groan of God in the hearts of men and women. And you need never despair for our wayward race while "the spirit himself maketh intercession for us with groanings which cannot be uttered."

Is the groan in the heart of God the answer to the groan in creation? What, you may well ask, of the tiger, the snake, and the floods I mentioned earlier and the many other happenings in the universe not easily traceable to human sin? Had Paul any answer to that?

Well, I can tell you what he *said*. You may not find it easy to follow his thinking. You may, indeed, say that he makes the assertion yet offers no reasons, but you must take that up with him! (It is my business to expound Paul, not to improve him!) One thing you can't say. You can't say that he doesn't *face* things.

Paul bound sinful humanity and the groaning universe together. He said that when man is free from sin, the agony of the universe will be over. Take the most especial heed of verse twenty-one in this eighth chapter of Romans. Creation itself is to be delivered from the bondage of corruption!

Have you ever wondered what God's ultimate intention is for this world? Is it just (as Keats called it) a "vale of soul making," having no purpose but to serve as a school for this human life and destined to destruction when that task is fulfilled? Some people think so. They compare it to the sand castles we build with the children on the seashore. What labor we expend on them to get the towers and the turrets and the moat all perfect, and the moment our back is turned the incoming tide begins to flatten it all again.

But the labor isn't lost, we say. The real purpose wasn't a sand castle but to nourish the health of the children, and while the sun and the breeze beat upon their half-bare bodies, the important work was being done. The sand castle can go. The physical fitness of the children was our real aim!

Is that all the world is?—a sand castle?

Some people think so and quote II Pet. 3:10 to prove that it will all disappear some day in "fervent heat."

Other Bible students—and they are ready with their quotations also—believe that the universe will have its place (by transformation) in eternity too. They believe that the birds and the beasts and the fish and all natural forces will share in God's redemption of our wayward race. Indeed, there are times when they even think they glimpse (as from afar) that blessed time of God's intention.

I traveled one day by air across half the United States. Leaving the far west, I looked down on a burned-up area and was surprised to see one range of hills beautifully cultivated on one side but with sterile desert on the other. I remarked on the contrast to a gentleman on the plane.

"Well," he said, "by nature, this area is *all* desert, though it is subject to occasional and drastic floods. They've just caught the floods in the reservoirs and, by the stored water, have irrigated one whole side of the range."

As easy as that! The flood had been redeemed.

When I landed from the plane, I had to continue my journey by car, and I was astonished to pass through an area which appeared to be covered by snake farms. Notice after notice was reared against the roadside: "Snake Farm."

I said to my kind host, who was driving, "Do you *farm* snakes here? We only kill them. What are they farmed for?"

"A number of reasons," he answered, "and some of them odd. But perhaps the most important is for medical purposes. Snake venom has healing values for the pharmacist."

Snake venom has value in healing! Is that *true?* Is the rattler then to be redeemed—and the cobra out at the penitent form!

It is a parable and a parable which recurred to my mind when, back in England, I visited the atomic center at Calder Hall. No bombs here! They are feeding electricity into the national grid. A scientist said to me, "You don't *have* to make bombs with nuclear power. Turned to peaceful uses, we could, by this means, take the ice Cap from the North Pole and open the Arctic Ocean to commerce. We could make the Sahara blossom like the rose, and we could landscape the universe! Is nuclear power to be redeemed?

Trust God! Be thankful for the realism of his apostle. This is not faith nourished on ignorance and deliberately blind to the ugly agonizing realities of this suffering world.

Face the facts as they are. Hothouse religion which can only maintain its tenuous life by ignoring challenging things will not do.

Hear the groan of creation. Hear the groan within yourself.

Hear, with exciting wonder, the Spirit making intercession for us with groanings which cannot be uttered.

Three groans!

God's last word is not a groan, but joy, joy, *joy!*

11

The Hands of Jesus Christ

In his hands the print of the nails . . .—John 20:25

I WANT TO SPEAK ABOUT HANDS AND, IN PARTICULAR, ABOUT THE hands of Jesus Christ. Our hands are no more important in one sense than any other part of our bodies—each part depending upon every other. And yet I think it is possible to assess the *special* importance of our hands from the way in which the word has crept into our speech and made a place for itself which is all its own.

The hands have been called "the executive officers of the brain"—and worthily they live up to that description. "To lend a hand" is a fine expression of service; "to be a poor hand" at anything is definite condemnation; "to come cap in hand" is a sign of servility; "to be an old hand" is a mark of ripe experience; "to come with an empty hand" is a sign of poverty or meanness; "to rule with a heavy hand" is to be an oppressor; to call a man your "right hand" is to make him your first assistant; "to get one's hand in" is to become familiar with the work; "to take a thing in hand" is to make it a serious undertaking; "to act with a high hand" is to be arrogant; "to have clean hands" is to be incorruptible; "to have one's hands full" is to be completely occupied; "to be a handful" is to be a nuisance; "to wash one's hands of a thing" is to abandon it entirely; "all hands on deck" is the cry in an hour of danger; "hands off" is a serious warning not to be ignored, and "hands up!" is the cry of the gangster which all but paralyzes his victim.

When we turn to things spiritual, the repetitive use of that fine word strikes us again. Our Lord told us that when we did good, we were to do it stealthily and not let our left hand know what our right hand was doing. And the psalmist said long ago that those who "ascend into the hill of the Lord" are those who have "clean hands and a pure heart."

I am bold to say that no other part of our body has so worked itself into common speech. Our five senses are inferior to those of the lower creatures. We have not an eye as sharp as the eagle's nor a nose as keen as the dog's. We have not an ear as alert as the horse nor a touch as sensitive as a spider's, but we outsoar all the lower creatures with our hands. Not even the ape can claim to have our amazing dexterity with hands.

Notice, also, that the word has not only worked itself into common speech; it has worked itself into custom and symbol as well. To shake hands is a sign of friendship. When I marry people, I bid them take their vows holding hands. When I was ordained to this ministry, hands were laid on my head.

Our hands are seldom idle. At work or play they are still serving us. Have you ever looked at your hands and thought on their thousand services to you through twenty, thirty, fifty, seventy years? When I meet a master pianist, when I talk with a brilliant surgeon, when I discuss a point with a skilled masseur, I love to look at their hands. What skill, what beauty, and what healing in those hands. When I take the service of Holy Communion, I do not see faces; I only see hands. How I exult in their variety, all reaching out for the bread which is his body and the wine which is his blood, all making their mute demand for that which Jesus will not deny: the large hands of men, the small hands of women, the smooth hands of the clerk, the rough hands of the manual worker, the soft hands of the woman of leisure, the coarse hands of those who have found life hard, the shapely hands of the maiden, and the shriveled hands of the old —all different and all equal at the table of the Lord. What interesting members of our bodies are our hands! I ask again, have you ever sat and looked at them? I do not want to take a deep dive into doctrine but you will follow me while I lead you in a simple meditation on the hands of Jesus Christ?

I

Will you notice, in the first place, that they were *toil-worn* hands. The soldier noticed it, the soldier who nailed him to the wood. As he stretched his arm along the crossbeam and pointed his nail at the palm, it struck him—this was not the hand of some sedentary worker; this was not the hand of some habitué of the court. This was the toil-worn hand of a working man.

Notice that! Jesus was a working man. Oh! you don't realize the wonder of that until you think yourself back into the Greek and Roman world and consider their attitude to manual work. They *despised* it. It was the occupation of slaves. Plato and Aristotle were both great and clever men, but to both of them manual work was a thing of near contempt. It was not an occupation for freemen; it was a task only for the slave.

And this was God's answer to that, his reply to the ancient world's contempt for manual work. Peep into the carpenter's shop at Nazareth, and see the incarnate Son of God bending his back at a bench; see him ankle-deep in the shavings and perspiring as he toils. This is the answer of almighty God to those who despise manual work.

Some of that pagan spirit has come down, alas, into the modern world. Have you noticed how we value people by their occupation? If a girl gets engaged to be married, if a new neighbor moves into your street, if you make a fresh acquaintance, almost the first question you ask about the fresh acquaintance, the new neighbor, or the boy to whom the girl is engaged is this: "What is he? And when you say, "What is he?" you mean, "What is his occupation? At what does he work?"

"He is a lawyer," or "He is a butcher (but in a big way!)" or "He is a bricklayer," and you can tell from the monosyllabic comments that are made afterwards just what the reaction is. Phew! A bricklayer!

In the subtle snobbery of our social life people fall into categories by their occupations. People forget that virtue is the only nobility. They graduate their respect not according to the quality of a man's life but according to the character of his occupation, and all their judgments are built on that basis. It is not many years since the daughter of a prime minister got engaged to an interior decorator. I know nothing about the interior decorator, and that she afterwards became the proprietoress of a pub is not a thing I want to comment on at this moment. I mention it merely for this. When the announcement was first made to the press, I overheard on the train two women who had just read that scrap of unimportant news.

"Well," said one to the other, "I thought she would have had somebody better than that!"

Think of it! She knew nothing about him but his occupation. He might have been a block of the salt of the earth, but her only comment was to wonder why the prime minister's daughter had nobody "better than that."

Jesus Christ was a working man. Remember the holy boldness of that verse of Charles Wesley:

> Son of the carpenter, receive
> This humble work of mine;

Worth to my meanest labour give,
By joining it to Thine.

I have heard townspeople speak sometimes contemptuously of farm laborers as "ignorant hobbledehoys" and display their own ignorance in so doing, for a farm laborer is a highly skilled man. Almost *all* his work is skilled work. The average townsman, used only to paving stones, would not know how to walk across a plowed field with a truss of hay on the end of a fork. What a strange survival of old-fashioned snobbery it is that we should accord a higher respect to a man of leisure who does no part of the world's work and call him a "gentleman" and, at the same time, deny respect to a man who bends his back and coarsens his hands as he takes his part of the labor of our race.

That is the first fruit I would like from this meditation. Think of the dignity of human labor. See it in the toilworn hands of Jesus Christ.

II

Not only was our Lord's hand a toil-worn hand; it was a *tender* hand. Both, and both together! And why not? Hands can be toil-worn and tender too. A hand can be tender without being soft!

When I was in Liverpool recently I heard, with dismay, of the damage that had been done by bombing to the cathedral. Apparently, it is only blast. But among the windows which have suffered is the window near the entrance to the Lady Chapel dedicated to some of the wonderful women of our race. It would interest you to see that window! Florence Nightingale, the noble nurse, is there, and Susanna Wesley, the mother of John and Charles; Josephine Butler, who fought the white-slave traffic, is there, and Grace Darling—in popular esteem the heroine of the Farne Islands. Those noble women are crowded together in one window, and I think, if you are a well-informed person, you would know them all—except perhaps one! Let me try her name out on you now to see how many of you know it. In that window of wonderful women Kitty Wilkinson finds place. Kitty Wilkinson!

"And who was Kitty Wilkinson?" you ask.

Ah! I feared you would not know. She was the saint of charwomen. I have a picture of her in my study. Her lovely life is little known beyond Liverpool, but they know it there, and she has a place in that wonderful window. When the cholera came to Merseyside, and everybody who could do so had fled, she stayed and fought the cholera, becoming the foster mother to forty-five orphaned children and earning their keep by washing and scrubbing in other people's homes.

She was the pioneer of the public washing-house. The first one that was ever opened in the country was opened by the authorities as a result of her influence. In my picture of Kitty Wilkinson it shows her hands. They are gnarled and shapeless. Forgive the word—they are "knobbly" and swollen at the joints. They look like the hands of one who was being beaten by rheumatism. But what tender hands! These are the hands of the woman who mothered the motherless; these are the hands our blessed Lord himself used in the slums of Liverpool more than a century ago.

Our Lord's hands were tender as well as toil-worn. They caressed the heads of little children.

I wish that His hands had been placed on my head!

They touched to life the little daughter or Jairus and stole the fever from the throbbing brows of Peter's mother-in-law. They touched the lepers and made them clean.

My friends, there may be those among you sad at heart today and sorely needing the tender touch of your Saviour's hands. Go to him in the quietness and ask his help in your need. Be unhurried. Wait before him, filled with just that longing—to find him near. And he will honor your faith. *He will touch you with his tender hand.*

III

Toil-worn, tender and—*pierced*. Have you ever seen a pierced hand—really looked at it? I had a little sister once, smitten by a vicious disease and operated upon so many times that her "visage was more marred than any man's," and she had to be hidden from the sight of all but the brave. Among her many disfiguring wounds was a pierced hand. I have many times sat and held it in mine. Even as a lad, taking my first faltering steps to personal faith, it reminded me of the Saviour's hand. It was like a poor, dumb mouth. What would it say if it could speak? What would the wounds of Jesus say? I found myself amending Shakespeare, and in my boyish perplexity murmuring, "I would there were a tongue in every wound of Jesus . . ." what would it say?

I know now. He would say, "*I have suffered.*"

Think of *that*, those of you who have suffered and those of you who suffer still. The hardest part of suffering for Christians is the dark hour when they are tempted to believe that God is not with them in it, when they suppose that Jesus reigns in some far-off splendor, untroubled by their woe. It is not true! I can testify that the first thing he does when he comes to the sufferers is to show them his hands. What a password! When you are pouring out your passionate protests to Jesus and asking him why this should happen to you, look! He is showing you his hands. Who should speak if he can't? The mystery still hangs, but who has suffered like the Saviour, and where is there such consolation as in his wounds?

When Paul went into prison, chained hand and foot, it must

have seemed a dark mystery that God should allow such a thing, seeing that Paul's only ambition was to preach about Jesus wherever he went. But, when he went to Jesus about it, I fancy that Jesus showed Paul his hands. That was enough! There is a kinship among those who suffer which others cannot share. They understand each other! Most talk on suffering by those who haven't suffered is shallow. And the Leader of the scarred company has pierced hands.

As we come to the conclusion of our meditation, I want you to think for a moment on the nail, the nail that pierced his hand. Have you ever wanted a symbol for sin? That nail would serve as well as anything.

Ask yourself this question. What would the hand of Jesus have been doing if it had not been nailed to the wood? It would have been moving out in blessing. It was always moving out in blessing. It moved out to heal, to soothe, to help.

That is what sin always does. It nails the hand of God. Sin beheaded Paul. Sin burned John Huss. Sin flung Bunyan into prison. Sin nails the tender hand of God.

If we could pull that nail out, what would the hand do? It would move out instantly to bless. And, in this world, he has no hands now but yours and those of other consecrated souls, who give their hands to him. That is the way to outwit sin. That is how to make the nail of no effect, to give him these hands, to say in simple truth:

> Take my hands and let them move
> At the impulse of Thy love.

So let us sit a few moments in silence looking at our hands and asking, "Are these the hands of Jesus Christ?"

12

The Pain of Answered Prayer

The twilight that I desired hath been turned into trembling unto me—Isa. 21:4

THERE IS A GOOD DEAL OF DISAGREEMENT AMONG SCHOLARS AS TO the exact historical background of this text, the precise period to which it belongs, and its full meaning. Yet we can understand, I think, the prophet's mind and enter, in some degree, into his feelings while those problems still remain unsolved.

The circumstances were these. The prophet desired light on the political situation of his day—which was always, of course, a religious matter to a Hebrew prophet, as well as a political one. He asked God to give him insight and vision that he might see what was hidden from the eyes of other men. He prayed for a divine illumination whereby his gaze might pierce the unknown future and his tongue foretell the prospects of his race. And —God gave the light! The prayer was answered! The darkness yielded to a growing twilight. He saw, but what he saw filled his soul with horror. He knew, but almost wished he did *not* know. The light glimmered all around him, but the pain of its revelation tempted him to plunge back into the darkness of ignorance again.

He saw the people he loved broken by the might of the enemy. He saw the homes and palaces and temple of his folk

shattered by the most ruthless of foes. God had answered his
prayer and given him the insight he desired, but he turned from
it sick with foreboding and with limbs that quivered in fearful
anticipation. He says, "The twilight that I desired hath been
turned into trembling unto me."

I

That is not an uncommon experience in the religious life. We
hear a great deal about the pain of *unanswered* prayer. What
about the pain of *answered* prayer? What about the light that
blisters and burns?

The answer our prayers receive is not always the answer our
hearts desire. He who asks God for light must not complain if
the light scorches at times with its fierce and naked heat. He
who pleads with God for guidance must not be surprised if he
points them to paths that they would rather not tread.

Oliver Wendell Holmes says that it is a rule which admits of
few exceptions that when folk ask for our opinion they really
want our praise.

God will not deal with us like that. If we plead for his light,
he will give it. He is too eager for our highest good to deny us the
healing truth. The truth—even if it hurts!

When the desire for soul peace awoke in the heart of Augustine, he turned to God and asked for divine light on the dark
problems of his way. And God gave the light, but the first thing
it revealed was Augustine's unchastity and incontinence. He
might well have said, "The twilight I desired hath been turned
into trembling unto me."

You remember the rich young ruler? "Good master, what must
I do to inherit eternal life?" And Jesus said, "Go, sell what thou
hast, and give to the poor, and thou shalt have treasure in heaven:
and then come and follow me."

But the young man loved his wealth. It was the first thing in his life. That was why Jesus condemned it. The first place in any man's life is God's place. The ruler might well have said, "The twilight I desired. . . ."

Nor is this experience peculiar only to those who are unsurrendered to Christ. Christian men know it, too.

When Thomas Champness was first appointed district evangelist to Newcastle-on-Tyne, he reconsecrated himself to God and asked for counsel at this new milestone in his life. And God gave him counsel! He said, "If you are to concentrate exclusively on winning men to me, you must be careless of your reputation as a preacher."

Ah! there's the rub at once. Every evangelist knows, especially if he has a scholar's brain and a scholar's heart, what sacrifices he must make for his evangelism. Outside the Church, the evangelist is often regarded as a humbug or (at the best) deluded, and inside the Church he is often sneered at as a "hot-gospeler." Certainly he exposes himself to the charge of being shallow-minded, though he may be (like Dwight L. Moody) a man with a first-class brain. He will be regarded by some as a dealer in unintelligent emotionalism, though his mind, like that of John Wesley, may be of logic all compounded.

Mrs. Hugh Price Hughes was once asked what was the greatest sacrifice her husband ever made, and she said, "He could have been a scholar but he chose, under God, to be a simple preacher of the gospel."

You may not think that a very great sacrifice, but that would only prove that you have not the scholar's heart. The greatest sacrifice some men have made for evangelism has been to obey the voice of God when he called them to abandon the delights of scholarly research and tell plain people, in plain words, the things which belong to their peace.

And God said to Thomas Champness, who had his own modest temptation to resist in that way, "If you want to concentrate on winning men to me, you must be careless of your reputation as a preacher." And Thomas Champness had a reputation in those days as a preacher—a reputation of which he was mildly proud. And God said, "Give it up!" The twilight he desired . . . !

You take a certain risk when you turn to God for guidance. You expose yourself to certain unsuspected possibilities. He is so fiercely intolerant of sin; he is so passionate for our highest good that he may tell us things we had almost rather not have known.

Yet to turn to God for light is of all things in the world the wisest thing any man or woman could do. You never know yourself until you see yourself in him.

II

Indeed, that is one of the greatest services our blessed Lord ever renders to our poor lost race, but be *prepared for the pain of it.* He shows men and women *themselves.* Jesus Christ falls in with a man, and that man's smug complacency vanishes like dew in the scorching heat of the sun. A divine dissatisfaction invades that contented soul.

Consequently, men react to him in different ways. I have known men who positively disliked him because he exposed them to themselves, because he drove them out from the snug retreat of low contentments and made them face the locked chambers of their own heart. You can pose to the world. God will not let you pose to him.

Have you ever heard of the Elephant Man? He was, perhaps, the most terrible monstrosity known in Europe in modern times. With a head as big around as a man's waist, he had what appeared to be the beginnings of a trunk and one abortive tusk, and only the strong-nerved could see him and not shudder. Sir Frederick Treves, the distinguished author and surgeon, in whose kindly care the Elephant Man spent the last years of his life, had an iron rule that no mirror of any kind ever be allowed in the Elephant Man's room. In that grotesque body there dwelt, as Treves discovered, a shy and sensitive soul. "At all costs," said Sir Frederick, "he *must* not see himself."

There is no counterpart to that in the spiritual world. There is no one of us whom God will shield from the truth. He holds up the mirror of Jesus before us, and, when we see ourselves in him, we see the poverty of our service and gauge the measure of our sin. Hence the absurdity of turning in anger or cowardice away from him. He is only the *mirror*. The impurities are all in us.

I have read somewhere of a British scientist in India who, years ago, was greatly troubled by the Hindu custom of drinking the water of the sacred river Ganges. He knew the water was full of impurities and most harmful to those who persisted in taking it. He wondered what he could do to stop the stupid practice. So he arranged an experiment and invited a leading Hindu priest, supposing that if he could only show the good man conclusively what foul drinking water it was, the priest would use his influence to save his people from disease.

And the day came. By means of powerful glasses the scientist magnified the foreign bodies in the water and invited the priest to look through the eyepiece and see what dreadful dangers were there. It was terrible water. It was like the water Kipling mentions in *Gunga Din*. "It was crawling, green, and stunk." But in the midst of the examination, when the scientist turned his back to get another specimen glass, swift as thought, the Hindu priest snatched the apparatus from the bench and dashed it in a dozen pieces on the floor. It was the answer of ignorance and bigotry to the healing light. He smashed the instrument—but he had not cleansed the water!

You can turn your back on Christ when he puts his finger on something in your life he does not approve, but, by turning your back, you have not cleansed your heart, nor has the peace of God seeped into your soul, nor has the joy and zest of life given you distinction among your fellows. When we make terms with Christ, they are *his* terms we must make, and every one of them is shaped for our progress in holiness.

I remember upsetting a woman once by a sermon. I had tried to teach the congregation, in a series of sermons, how to go to God for guidance, and in the last of the series I pleaded with them to put him to the test.

This woman did not appear at church for some weeks, and when we met, she told me that she had taken my advice. I feared for a moment that no guidance had been given.

"What happened?" I asked anxiously. "Did you hear nothing?"

"Oh," she said, "it came to me that I ought to write to my sister-in-law (*the cat!*) with whom I quarreled seven years ago. *I won't do that . . .*"

"This is the judgment, that light is come into the world, and men loved the darkness rather than the light."

III

There is but one thing we can do when we tremble in the blinding light of new revelation. We must go into the light with God. *Pain or no pain, march on.*

There is no going back—*not in heart.* The comfort of ignorance has gone for good. You *can* slip back if you will, but you have *seen* the light, and it has stolen your peace forever.

Augustine tried to run away, you remember, but he was driven out of every refuge until he found refuge in him.

The rich young ruler turned back, but notice that he turned back *sorrowful*.

Why didn't he laugh in our Lord's face and say, "Give up all my money? Do you think I'm a fool . . . ?"

No! The light had done its work. He had seen the truth, and peace had gone. I am bold to say that he was haunted by the face of Jesus till the day he died.

Christ is our rightful Lord. Our peace is in his keeping. There is a deep homing instinct in our hearts which runs out to him as soon as he truly appears. Augustine knew why. He "has formed us for himself, and our hearts are restless till they find rest in him."

You must do what Champness did. You must accept his terms. It is the way of wisdom and the way of peace. When God said to Thomas Champness, "If you want to be just an evangelist in Newcastle you must be careless of your reputation as a preacher," he struggled, but he yielded. Speaking of the effort it cost him later, he said, "I threw my reputation as a preacher into the Tyne as I crossed the high-level bridge." God made him a glorious harvester of souls.

Men and women, pray for the light! But remember, the light may reveal more than you wish. It may be turned into trembling unto you.

Yet I plead with you, by all the force I can command, not to parley now. If you will live up to the demands that he makes, if you will face squarely what that light reveals, if you will do what he says, the trembling will pass; you will prove the power of God to strengthen the weak hands and confirm the feeble knees. You will be led into green pastures, with peace in your heart, and in your enlarging spiritual effectiveness you will know one more of the many reasons why the apostle said, "Walk in the light."

13

Ambassadors for Christ

We are ambassadors for Christ, as though God did
beseech you by us: we pray you in Christ's stead, be
ye reconciled to God—II Cor. 5:20, K.J.V.

DID YOU EVER READ THAT REMARKABLE BOOK CALLED *Ambassador
on Special Mission?* It was written by Lord Templewood, still
best known to most people as Sir Samuel Hoare. It tells the
story of his dispatch to Spain at a most critical period of the late
war with instructions to keep Franco out of the struggle, and it
tells something also of the adventures which befell him in that
difficult task.

As I followed the twists and turns of fortune and of policy
and sensed again the privileges and responsibilities of the ambassador's life, I remembered once more those striking words of
Paul, "We are ambassadors for Christ." I would like to examine
these words with you.

I

Everybody knows—even the least informed—that an ambassador is one who represents his own country in an alien land. If
his country is a monarchy, the ambassador is regarded as the
personal representative of the king (or queen), and it is expected
that he will be accredited the honors and distinctions which be-

long not to him as a person but to the one in whose place he stands.

Not only is the ambassador regarded as the personal representative of his king, but his official residency, the embassy, is always accounted as belonging not to the country in which it is built but to the country to which the ambassador himself belongs. The British Embassy in Washington is a little bit of Britain. The American Embassy in London is a precious scrap of the United States.

Within the walls of an embassy only those rules and customs and laws are observed which belong to the land of the ambassador; the laws and the customs of the alien land in which he lives pass by unheeded. When America went "dry," there was still wine on the table of the British Ambassador in Washington— and the Ambassador was not breaking the law. Britain had not gone dry! On the fourth Thursday of every November there is a wonderful party at the American Embassy in Grosvenor Square in London because it is Thanksgiving Day. But Thanksgiving Day has no place in the British calendar, and all around the rest of Mayfair is just November!

An ambassador's allegiance is to his own land and his own king. He dwells as a Britisher (or American) *in* Spain or Portugal or in the Argentine, but he is not *of* it. His citizenship and his loyalty and his love are all elsewhere.

"Now," says Paul, "we are ambassadors for Christ."
Ambassadors! Personal representatives of our heavenly King.

> Chosen to be soldiers
> In an alien land.

And more than soldiers—ambassadors!

Chosen, called, and faithful,
For our Captain's band.

Is that true? Are you living up to your ambassadorial status?

No one sensitive to the importance of rank can ever speak lightly of the ambassadorial status. It is, in all conscience, a tremendous thing to be the personal representative of a great ruler and to speak for your whole land.

Would you like to have been the ambassador of Britain to Turkey when the poor Samaritans were being exterminated and to have told the Sultan to his face, "My queen won't stand aside and see this little people wiped out"? There are Samaritans in the world today because the ambassador said that!

Would you like to have been the ambassador of Britain to Portugal after the dreadful disaster at Lisbon in 1755 and to have said to the King of Portugal, "My king commands me to convey his deep compassion to you and to your people and to give you forty thousand pounds to alleviate the distress."

It is a high office, the office of an ambassador. Are you living up to your status? Are you really an ambassador of Jesus Christ?

And tell me this. Is your home an embassy of heaven?

That is what Paul asked his beloved Philippians when he wrote to them. Philippi had the distinction of being a Roman colony with all the privileges which that status carried in the ancient world, but Paul wanted the church at Philippi to be a colony of heaven.

Is this church, so far as you can make it, a colony of heaven? Is your home, so far as you can make it, an embassy of Jesus Christ? Do *his* rules and customs and laws alone prevail within its walls? Is service the motive and peace the atmosphere and joy the sunshine and love the whole reward? If some discerning soul called on you at home, would he say within himself, "This is an embassy of Jesus Christ"?

II

Now an ambassador always has, as one of his jealously guarded privileges, *direct access to the king* (or president) *he represents.* How could he possibly represent his king unless he knew the monarch's mind?

Consequently, it is the established practice among all civilized communities which maintain ambassadors in the capital cities of other powers to guarantee to every ambassador uninterrupted communication with those he represents.

Our post office carries the diplomatic mailbag of every ambassador accredited to the Court of St. James, but never, on the solemn word of Britain, is that mailbag ever opened and explored. It cannot be tampered with by the civil service, nor by Scotland Yard, nor by the customs and excise authorities, nor by any others.

The same respect is paid to the mailbags of our own ambassadors abroad. They are sealed at the foreign office, and with the seal unbroken, they are delivered in Paris, Brussels, Rome, Madrid, and wheresoever else our ambassadors reside.

No man would accept his high office if he were not guaranteed uninterrupted communication with his king.

The Christian ambassador is guaranteed no less. When Jesus Christ makes us ambassadors, he promises us that indispensable privilege. He says, "You are going to represent me in an alien world. You may always know my mind. Nothing need ever interrupt our intercourse *but your neglect or indifference.* When you pray, I will hear; when you listen, I will speak. Nothing external to yourself can ever cut our communications. You may always know the mind of your King."

So the Christian ambassadors have proved all through the ages. They flung John Bunyan into prison—but they couldn't cut his communications. In prison he prayed, and God heard him. In prison God spoke, and Bunyan knew his King's mind.

George Fox and John Nelson and Samuel Rutherford and a thousand others have been incarcerated in jail for Christ's sake, but they all testified that the mail arrived from heaven; they had sweet communion with their King.

I was speaking once to one of our boys recently home from the war. He was telling me—what I knew by experience already— of the problems of living the Christian life in the services.

"The secret of success," he said, "is in prayer. If I could get away for a quiet time, if I could speak to God and listen to God, all was well."

That is the secret of success in the ambassadorial service any-where and at any time.

Do you know why so many people fail as Christian ambassadors? They don't maintain communication with their King.

But Lord Templewood, in his recent book, stressed something else beside that. He said that if an ambassador stays too long in the country to which he is accredited—that is to say, if he does not make fairly frequent visits to his own land and breathe his own native air—he gets "denationalized."

The process can go on, it seems, without the ambassador being fully aware of it. When he first arrives on his mission, he is British or American through and through. To the discerning eye, "made in England" or "made in America" is written all over his face. He sees things his own way, assesses them from his own standpoint, is able, even in a land of dictators, to see things always from the democratic angle.

But, half-unconsciously, there supervenes a cosmopolitan way of looking at things. The atmosphere of the alien land gets into his lungs. Whenever he goes out, he meets people of *that* land. Whenever he talks, he hears the viewpoint of *those* people expressed. Bit by bit—and almost imperceptibly at first—his attitude is affected; it begins to change. From British or American it becomes cosmopolitan, pro-Spanish or Italian or Brazilian—whatever the country may be.

The problem of every ambassador, if he is to remain loyal to his commission, is to be true all the time to his prime allegiance.

And Lord Templewood says that, if he is to do that, he must "renew his strength by contact with his native soil," breathe his own atmosphere, talk with his own kind, and get truly orientated again from the center.

And how true that is of the Christian!

No man or woman can hope to be a dependable ambassador of Jesus Christ unless he or she maintains prime allegiance. The alien world in which we live affects us all. We are in it nearly all the time. Its judgments affect us; its atmosphere penetrates us; its pressures bear on us in ten thousand ways.

How easily, without realizing it, do we become what the apostle calls "conformed to this world." How easily we accept a lower standard, take to saying, "Well, I see no harm in it," lose the sharp distinction between right and wrong, have all our blacks and whites dissolve into one indeterminate grey, keep up the pretence of being ambassadors by preserving one or two Christian customs. But for the rest we are unworthy, quite definitely not true to our ambassadorial status, something of a failure, a casualty of the diplomatic service.

Is that true of you? Dare you say with Paul, "I am an ambassador for Christ"?

How can one save oneself from being what Lord Templewood calls "denationalized" and what, in this connection, I may call "despiritualized"? By what means can a man be on his guard against that possibility?

You must do what Templewood did. You must get back whenever you can to your own atmosphere. You must mingle, at every opportunity, with your own kind. You must guard not only your own mailbag—by which I mean those secret communications you may have in private prayer and in listening to God— but you must also keep in the Christian fellowship, be found often in the sanctuary, count Sunday to Sunday too long in the atmosphere of the world, and seek a meeting of fellowship or prayer in the mid-week.

I believe that ambassadors can retain their true citizenship in this alien world without those meetings of mid-week fellowship if they are always jealously guarding their periods of daily prayer and if it is quite impossible for them to get to those mid-week meetings at all.

But if you are serious to maintain your ambassadorial status, and if it is possible for you to get to a week-day class or Christian fellowship meeting or prayer group, oh, I beg of you, be there. Be there!

III

You will remember that I remarked, as I began, that Lord Templewood described himself as "an ambassador on special mission." He was not an ordinary ambassador. His king set him a specific task.

England was at a grim phase of the war. She was hard-pressed. She was, indeed, alone in the fight against tyranny. The Nazis were supreme from the Pyrennes to Russia, and some, even of our staunch American friends, doubted if we could possibly hold out.

Franco was known to be pro-Nazi and pro-Fascist. He made

no secret of it himself. He identified himself with those evil régimes and openly announced himself as simply "non-belligerent."

Lord Templewood, in that hour of need, was sent to keep him out of the war, to prevent his coming in militantly on the side of the Axis. For if the Germans had swept down the Iberian Peninsula, how would it have gone with the handful of men on the Rock of Gibraltar, who would have had but little choice except to sell their lives dearly and see the Mediterranean sealed at its western end?

Those of us who followed events closely in those days felt almost sure, during some months, that Franco would come in against us.

He never came in against us! Let Lord Templewood have his credit for that. He set himself the task of understanding the Spanish mind, of thinking their thoughts before them, of putting our case and keeping them out.

He was, indeed, an ambassador on special mission. It would have gone ill with Britain if Spain had come in against us then.

But we, as Christian ambassadors, have a special mission too: indeed, none so special as we are!

Remember the whole text. This is how Paul put it: "Now then we are ambassadors for Christ, as though God did beseech you by us; we pray you in Christ's stead, be ye reconciled to God."

"Be ye reconciled to God!" What a task! Have you felt the critical character and all the responsibility and importance of your mission as ambassadors of reconciliation?

I said just now that Lord Templewood studied the Spanish mind, and Franco's in particular. He was very lonely; the embassy was sometimes mobbed, and he had no firm friend but the American ambassador—so he concentrated the more on the Spanish mind.

Do you study the minds of people outside the Church—and in particular, the people you know?

Templewood had to ask himself, "What do they want? What do they fear? How can I put my point of view in such a way that they will follow my counsel?"

Do you ask those things about the worldling? "What does he want? What does he fear? How can I put my plea in such a way that he himself will want to be reconciled to God?"

When he says to you, "I want to get a kick out of life. I want to be happy," do you know how to tell him about a joy that never fades away, happiness that has no hangover? Can you tell him about that?

When he says that he wants satisfaction and thinks that the way to satisfaction is to give his animal desires whatever they want whenever they want it, do you know how to convince him that that is the way to a troubled conscience, and that only in God can he find a peace that endures?

I am asking you *this*, in short; do you know the craft of this ambassadorial skill in personal evangelism? Can you clear misunderstandings from the unbeliever's mind and tell him convincingly and without embarrassment, "I am from God. Oh, yes! I hold that status. I am an ambassador of the King of kings. I have been commissioned from above. I am accredited to this alien world. I have letters patent to prove my ambassadorial status. The King I represent wants a reconciliation with you. Though he is the offended One, he takes the initiative, and he wants me to tell you that there are no barriers in him to that reconciliation. Whatever barriers there are, are all in you. If you want to be right with him, you can. He has provided the way. Accept the atonement of his only begotten Son. Put yourself within the newly covenanted mercies. Regularize your position in relation to heaven. He has pardon for you. Take the pardon. Be reconciled to God."

You wouldn't use that *language*. You would adapt it to the person you were addressing, but there would be no blurring of the sense. Your "special mission" is to get them reconciled to God, and you would have to take as direct a line to the end as you could.

What a mission! Oh, the privilege and wonder of being able to say it, of being able to say it to *anybody*, to know that it is for all—the foulest, the most inferior, the man who has murdered his mother even.

Tell it out! You are an ambassador. Tell it out! Live up to your ambassadorial status. Spend your days that way.

> 'Tis worth living for this,
> To administer bliss
> And salvation in Jesus's name.

IV

Sooner or later every ambassador is relieved of his post. He is called home. Lord Templewood was called home. His task had been well done. The king told him so, Sir Winston Churchill said so, and the discerning public said so too.

But doubtless it was the king's word that meant the most to him. And it was not a word of thanks only. He was rewarded. He was given a peerage and a place by the throne. The king said, in effect, "When the court is in session, stand here; stand by the throne. The work was well done, and I am well pleased."

Some day the Christian ambassador will be called home. God doesn't intend that he dwell forever in an alien land. Some day that call will come to you and to me. Suddenly perhaps—or with warning. It is as the Monarch wills. When it comes, may it only find us fulfilling our ambassadorial duties, busy in the tasks he has given, filling the moments with glad service to him.

Recently, in the town of Stockton-on-Tees, I went into a house to see an old ambassador of Jesus Christ waiting for his call home. He had been warned. I have known him for years. What an ambassador he has been! They know my friend along Teesside. Eighty-eight last week, but he has not been out of his room for a year, and, as I leaned over his bed, I said to him (remembering a favorite hymn) with a twinkle in my eye, "Is it well with thy soul?"

And he replied firmly and smilingly, "It is *well;* it is WELL with my soul."

He is waiting to be called home, that ambassador. He feels an unprofitable servant, but he sees also the smile of his King. He is not afraid. He is just waiting for the call.

Will it be like that with you some day? You hope to die in your bed and have time enough to recollect yourself before the journey is begun.

That is how I hope it will be with me. I hope, when he comes for me, that in some way or other I may be discharging my ambassadorial duties, and for myself and for you I would say:

> O that each in the day
> Of His coming may say:
> I have fought my way through,
> I have finished the work Thou didst give me to do!
>
> O that each from his Lord
> May receive the glad word:
> Well and faithfully done;
> Enter into My joy, and sit down by My throne!

14

A Freeman of the City

And the chief captain answered, With a great sum obtained I this freedom. And Paul said, But I was free born—Acts 22:28, K.J.V.

I READ IN THE NEWSPAPER THAT THE DUKE OF EDINBURGH HAD been given the freedom of the fine city from which he takes his title, and he can now say, both in London and in Edinburgh, "I am a freeman of the city."

It is a fine thing to be a freeman of a great city. Paul was a freeman of the city of Rome. That distinction carried with it certain high privileges.

No degrading punishment could be laid upon a freeman. He had the right of appeal to the emperor if he ever felt that he had been unjustly sentenced, and, if he was on a capital charge, he could claim to be tried by the emperor himself. More than once in his stormy career Paul had found it highly convenient to assert his Roman citizenship.

Here was a case in point. Paul had been arrested in Jerusalem as a disturber of the peace, and he proved to be one of the strangest prisoners the chief captain had ever taken into custody. He startled the captain first by addressing him in Greek, and the captain (who supposed he was an Egyptian) said, "Dost thou know Greek?"

When he was given permission to speak to the people, Paul further astonished the captain by addressing them in polished Hebrew. And when a riot broke out at the end of his speech and the captain ordered his prisoner to be whipped, Paul had a further surprise up his sleeve.

He said to the soldiers, "You can't scourge me! I am a Roman and uncondemned."

And when they called the chief captain, he came in astonishment and said, "Art thou a Roman?" And Paul said, "Yes." To which the captain answered, "With a great sum obtained I this freedom." And Paul said, "But I was free born."

My dear friends, I am going to tell you how to be a freeman of the city—a freeman of the city where you live and a freeman of the city of God (where I hope you will live for all eternity).

I

There are four ways by which you can become a freeman of the city of London. First, you can become a freeman by servitude —the way my old grandfather became a freeman of the city of London. Any male citizen of full age, on completion of his apprenticeship to a freeman, can become a freeman himself. You work your passage!

The old craftsmen's guilds were maintained that way. You became, by reason of your recognized skill, a member of the Mercers', the Vintners', the Drapers', or the Fishmongers' Company.

It was freedom by servitude; you spent your time, acquired your skill, and you were in.

There is no way into the city of God by servitude. You cannot work your passage to heaven. Men of rigorous morality have tried to do so in every age, but they have always failed.

There is no road that way. The Pharisees tried it. John Wesley tried it before his conversion. Misguided men and women are trying it still.

People outside the churches and uninstructed in evangelical religion often say, "No, I don't go to church, but I never miss the opportunity of doing someone a good turn. . . ."

They do not draw the inference in so many words, but it is there: "My good turns will get me into heaven, if there is a heaven to get into. Clearly, that is the place where I belong."

My dear friends, your good turns will not get you into heaven. At your finest you are an unprofitable servant.

There is something to be forgiven in the best things you ever do. If you put all your service into one scale—all your good turns and all your kind thoughts—and in the other scale your mean thoughts, your unkind words, your shabby motives, your gross self-centeredness and all your bad turns (which you have probably forgotten), can you doubt which way the scale would go down?

Can you not hear the righteous sentence: "Thou art weighed in the balance, and found wanting"?

One night years ago, I was preaching on personal religion. When the service ended, a scoutmaster came up to me. He told me, with moving frankness, that he didn't understand a thing I had been saying because he knew nothing of personal religion himself.

Yet he had known of this lack a long time. In his confusion, years before, he had said to himself, "I don't understand all this talk about personal religion, but it must be right to do good."

And so he had taken up the service of boys and done it with splendid devotion, but all the time with an aching feeling inside that he still didn't know the big secret of life and somehow was not right with God.

The obstacle came out in conversation! There was sin in his life which had to be faced and had to be forgiven.

It may be so with you.

I helped that scoutmaster by giving him an illustration of a friend of mine who said once:

Imagine a home with two children, a boy and a girl about the same age. One morning the boy does something unkind to his sister, strikes her savagely, maybe, and his mother notices it. A hurt look comes into her eyes. She has noticed this strain in her little son's character before, and none of her counsel seems to have eradicated it.

The little boy notices the hurt look in his mother's eyes, and he feels a sense of guilt within. He tries to put mother right by offering to do things for her.

"Can I go on any errands for you, Mummy? Do you want anything brought down from upstairs?"

He keeps offering his little services, but none of it takes the hurt look out of his mother's eyes.

All day they go on like that, and toward bed-time the little boy can stand it no longer. He runs to his mother, flings his arms around her neck, and says,

"I'm sorry, Mummy."

No need to explain what he's sorry about. They both know, and they have both been thinking about it all day.

"Are you really sorry, Son?" asked his mother, and adds her wise admonitory words.

And when she's sure he is sorry, he is kissed and forgiven, and she can think at once of half-a-dozen things she wants him to do.

"Run upstairs and get me so-and-so, dear. Do this for me; do that."

Oh, with what happy, eager steps he runs upon her errands. Nothing hinders him now. He is forgiven. He is right within.

How true that little analogy is. God says, "First my arms and then my errands." He says that to you now. Don't try to reverse the order. It will not do. To serve him without reconciliation is to rob the service of inwardness and true acceptability, and never, of itself, will it bring you perfect peace.

You can become a freeman of the city of London by servitude but not by that means a freeman of the city of God.

II

The second way in which you can become a freeman of the city of London is *by patrimony* or, as we should say, by birth. Any children of a freeman (male or female) can be "free" when they become of full age, if the father was free when they were born.

If their father obtained his freedom *after* their birth, it doesn't apply to them, but, provided he was free when they were born, they can claim the privilege on obtaining their majority, and the city fathers will honor the claim.

It is a grand thing to have a good father. It secures some people all kinds of privileges all through their life, and even if it doesn't secure great privileges, it often gives one a warm throb at the heart.

A couple of years ago I went to preach at an afternoon anniversary service.

As I left the building, I was accosted by a poor, old, well-spoken woman who timidly asked me if I was Dr. Sangster, and when I admitted that I was, she said, with some excitement. "I knew. You look so like him."

"So like whom, madam?" I asked.

"Your father," she said. "I worked for him years ago. Oh, sir, he was kind to me. . . . "

I think we had twenty minutes together. She couldn't tell me enough. I egged her on, and she grew reminiscent about my dear father.

It's lovely to hear your own good father praised, and it's good to think on all the fine things one's paternity has brought, but there is one thing the best father in the world cannot secure for you, and that is a guaranteed place in heaven.

142

Birth may be enough to make you a freeman of the city of London. Birth isn't enough for the city of God.

Hophni and Phinehas had a good father in Eli, but they did evil in the sight of the Lord, and they brought shame on all Israel.

Absalom had a good father, but he broke his father's heart and died a traitor's death in a rebellion. William Godwin was the son of a minister. Nothing is more certain that that their parents would have been pained by their subsequent lives.

How many times I have heard men, neglectful of the just claims of religion on them, asserting (as though it were warrant enough for their own future) that they had had a good father or a good mother!

I am glad to hear any man say that, but what of it?

You can become a freeman of the city of London by birth but not by that means a freeman of the city of God.

III

The third way by which you can become a freeman of the city is *by honorary presentation*. This was how the Duke of Edinburgh became a freeman both of London and of Scotland's capital as well. It was given him. It was by honorary presentation. This is the normal method in London.

The Court of Common Council of the city, meeting usually at the Guildhall, decide to honor some distinguished servant of the state, and they do so by bestowing the freedom of the city. It is the highest honor in the city's gift.

Normally, it is presented at a colorful function; eulogistic speeches are made, and the scroll is handed over in a beautifully wrought box. It is commonly believed that there is no more honorable way of becoming a freeman than by this honorary presentation—though everybody doesn't agree with that!

You cannot become a citizen of heaven by the honorary presentation of any council on earth—not even an ecclesiastical one! Human tribunals are all capable of error, and history is studded with judicial crimes.

The Athenian Council, in solemn conclave, voted upon the death of Socrates, that saint of paganism. Two hundred and twenty voted for his acquittal, 280 voted for his condemnation, and he was compelled to drink the hemlock as a man not fit to live.

Jesus was falsely condemned both by the ecclesiastical and the civil courts. Joan of Arc was burned after the same hollow process. Savonarola went to the stake with a similar official seal upon his unjust death.

Did you ever read the story of Savonarola? We have become, alas, familiar again with tortures and dubious confessions in our own age, and when Savonarola was arrested by order of the Pope, he was tortured day after day. In the extremity of his pain he confessed many things he had never done, but the moment the torture ceased he withdrew all the confessions again.

Yet the Pope said to the judges that Savonarola must die "even if he is a second John the Baptist."

When the time came for that brave man to be done to death, the awful service began, first, with his official degradation, but the bishop in charge of the proceedings slipped. Either out of bravado, or because he was flustered, he said more than he should have said.

The service required that he say, "I separate thee from the Church Militant," but he added also "and from the Church Triumphant."

As that second phrase fell from his lips, Savonarola flashed back: "That is beyond thy power."

It was indeed. There is no ecclesiastical court on earth which can exclude a man from the Church Triumphant. That judgment is for God alone. And just as no ecclesiastical court can exclude a man from the Church Triumphant, so no court on earth can put him in.

There is no conclave which can secure your entrance into heaven by any pronouncements, however solemn. The Church is sometimes said to "make saints," but that is a euphemism. Only God can make a saint and secure his place in glory.

You can become a freeman of the city of London by vote of the Court of Common Council, but neither the College of Cardinals, nor the Lambeth Conference, nor any other assembly of earth, can vote you into the city of God.

IV

How, then, can one become a citizen of heaven?

There is still another way of becoming a freeman of the city of London, and that will give us the clue that we are seeking.

You can become a freeman by servitude. You can become a freeman by birth. You can become a freeman by honorary presentation. Notice, finally, that you can become a freeman by redemption.

Oh, yes, that is the word! It has a religious sound, but it is a civic word as well. You can become a freeman of the city of London by "redemption"; that is the actual word the city fathers use.

Can I put it crudely—even if you don't like the way I put it? You can buy your way in. You could do that in ancient Rome. That was what the chief captain meant when he said, "With a great sum obtained I this freedom." He had bought his way in. Paul was a freeman by patrimony. That was why he answered, "But I was free born."

And you can buy yourself into the freedom of London (the

sum is quite nominal)—and listen, that is the only way you can become a freeman of the city of God—by redemption, by being bought in. Here is the clue we were seeking! This is the one way to the city of God.

Now, let us be clear what we mean by "being bought in." We are not suggesting for a moment, I need hardly say, that a man can reach the Holy City by some display of worldly wealth, by princely giving, even to good causes, or by the most prodigal generosity to the Church of God.

Paul says in Colossians, "We have redemption through his blood." I admit freely that something of mystery hangs over the divine decree that redemption and the shedding of blood are bound together, but they are, and you make nonsense of the Book of God and whole areas of normal life if you seek to divorce that solemn combination: redemption . . . and the shedding of blood.

Says Paul to the Corinthians, "Ye are not your own; ye were bought with a price." That is the most solemn and glorious fact of human existence. You are redeemed! The city of God is open to you. Accept, in penitence, the sacrifice made in your behalf, and nothing impedes you in claiming citizenship of that city whose builder and maker is God.

There are still people who feel that there is something vindictive in God that he should require the shedding of blood to redeem. They think it is crude and un-Godlike and savors more of the savageries of primitive peoples than the enlightened religion of Jesus Christ, nor do I deny our inability fully to explain the divine strategy in it all.

But how can there be anything of vindictiveness in a costly redemption *which God bore himself?* What he requires, he bears. "Something heavy must be paid"—but God says, "I pay it. . . ."

Can I make that still plainer to you by some simple illustration of the home, even though it has no reference to blood? We preachers sometimes put it like this.

Imagine a father who has a disobedient boy. Again and again, out of sheer naughtiness and willfulness, the boy disobeys his father's instructions, and finally his father says, "If you do that again, I'll make you spend the night in the attic."

And he does it again, and the father's integrity and truthfulness and firmness are all now dependent on his application of the punishment.

The boy must spend the night in the attic.

At eight o'clock, instead of going to his room and to his bed, he is sent to the attic, and his father sits by the fire downstairs.

Can he read? No! Can he lose himself in a hobby? No! Is he grateful for the warmth of the fire? No—it mocks him! Finally, at ten o'clock, he can stand it no longer. He will not remit the punishment. He cannot. But he goes up to the attic, and he spends the whole night there with his boy.

It is a silly illustration, you may think but, maybe, not so silly. By that simple means you may glimpse something of what it was with God.

"Apart from the shedding of blood there is no remission." Maybe we would never have known the real character of sin in all its devilish wickedness unless we had seen the sinless Son of God impaled upon the Cross. "Ye are not your own; ye were bought with a price."

Well? Do you want to be a freeman of the city of God? This is the way to it, the only way. Come in penitence; come and take the oath of allegiance, and he will meet your penitence with pardon, and henceforth you will be able to say, "My citizenship is in heaven. I am, indeed, a freeman of the city of God."

15

You Can't Make People Good

Prepare ye the way of the people; cast up, cast up the highway; gather out the stones; lift up an ensign.
—Isa. 62:10

IT IS IMPOSSIBLE TO make PEOPLE GOOD. I STRESS THE WORD "make." If it were possible to make people good, if virtue were ever the fruit of compulsion, then all that militant moralists would need to do would be to get the monarch to issue some imperial fiat or constrain Parliament to pass an act or formulate a local by-law and get it through the council, and the Golden Age could begin tomorrow. But it isn't possible to make people good.

In the exuberance of poetry or the enthusiasm of preaching, hymn writers and pastors sometimes speak as though it were possible to make people good. Charles Wesley sings:

> Thou canst, Thou wouldst, this moment save
> Both me and all mankind.

But the inference, all the time, is that the people are *willing* to be saved, and, if they are not willing, you cannot make them. Ebenezer Elliott's Chartist hymn is much beloved in some circles, but it is more than a little ridiculous for the same reason. It inquires:

> When wilt Thou save the people?
> O God of mercy, when?

The question is repeated. God, it would appear, is some deaf or indifferent or decidedly tardy deity, who will not do what is plainly expected of him.

"When wilt Thou save the people?" The answer is surely this: "Just as soon as ever the people are willing to be saved."

But you cannot make them willing—no, not even your brother or your friend or your son. Not him even! You cannot make him good. Out of the heart, fashioned in freedom, the fine fruit of constraint, though never of compulsion, arises this warm desire of the soul for what we call virtue. Precisely how God begets it in us and from what secret springs of aspiration he contrives that the waters rise, we do not know. This only we know. He does not compel us, and we cannot compel others. Far deeper than the surface thoughts which fret our mind, God conducts that holy traffic with our souls by which he saves us and makes us good.

Does it follow, then, that all our longings for a new world are vain and empty? Is it useless to spend our time and strength in work and prayer for a new order of things?

By no means! There is a great and essential task we have to do. Almighty God depends on our doing it. There is a high and holy work he has placed upon us all, and our failure will delay the purposes of the Almighty.

Let me make that clear by calling two witnesses who will set our duty plainly before us, one witness from our own times and one from an age gone-by.

Professor Bernard Bosanquet in his well-known book, *The Philosophical Theory of the State*, grappled with the very question we are considering now. He proposed these questions to his own mind: "What could the State do to make people good? Could it do anything? Could it do a lot?" And, necessarily, his argument ranged over these same areas of thought. Finally, he concluded with a declaration which some found very disappointing: that the only thing the State could do was "to hinder the hindrances to the good." That is to say, its great function was a negative one, that the desire for goodness, and the will to pursue it, had an origin beyond our control, and that all we could do was to clear the way of the things which might impede.

So said the modern philosopher.

The ancient prophet said no less.

Look at his circumstances for a moment. The long exile of the Jews was over. Royal permission had been given to them to return and rebuild their ruined city, and Zion awaited the coming of her dispossessed sons.

But it was not in the power of the prophet to compel the exiles to return. Babylon had proved a seductive city to many of them. They were doing well in business, and their commercial prospects were good. It was asking a great deal to invite them to leave a life which had elements of luxury and start again with next to nothing on those stern Judean hills.

The prophet knew the difficulty. He says, in effect, "We cannot force them to return. The city of God will seem very unattractive to some of them in comparison with Babylon, that center of sensuality, but though we cannot compel them to come, we can at least put a highway in between, a firm, metaled road, unimpeded by boulders, and as attractive as we can make it." "*Prepare ye the way of the people; cast up, cast up the highway; gather out the stones; lift up an ensign.*"

That is our task still.

Let us consider how best it can be done.

I

We gather out the stones when we have a Christian concern for social reform.

Those Christian people who take no interest in civic, social, or national affairs and defend their neglect on the ground that these matters have nothing to do with the marrow of religion are wrong—and tragically wrong. They forget the stern words of the Master concerning the scribes who preyed upon poor widows and thought they had concealed their wickedness because they prayed to God.

Social conditions matter. It is a Christian duty to fight injustice wherever it can be brought to battle. The plain material circumstances of life can aid or hinder folk on their journey to the Celestial City. It is gloriously true that God has had his saints in the most foul surroundings, but to twist that undisputed fact into a ground for supine indifference to conditions which impede the soul's aspirations is to sin against the light. It is easier to be a Christian in a garden city than in an odorous slum. Whatever makes it harder to believe in a God of love, whatever serves as an impediment to people in their struggle towards Christ, whatever blocks the way of those who "travel to the sky" is a stone. And we have received instructions about stones. We must gather them out!

When Beverley Nichols left Oxford, he says that he was full of socialistic ideals and felt it his plain duty to identify himself with the poor in their struggles. He went to Glasgow and tried to live on fifteen shillings a week. In those days of wide unemployment thousands of youths were compelled to do the same. He says, "I stayed in a miner's cottage for seven shillings, six pence a week which left me about one shilling a day for food and everything else. Even though I had my clothes and boots and my hair cut, I found I just couldn't do it. I was soon nervously run down and the poor diet made me break down altogether. In ten days I cracked up and came home very ill."

Think of it! In the conditions in which thousands of his fellow countrymen had to live for years, he broke down in ten days. It is the simple truth that the struggle for the bread of this life is so hard for many people that they have hardly time or spirit to struggle for the bread of any other.

It was a little before the outbreak of war in 1939, in a certain town in this country, and in the course of my pastoral visitation, that I visited a man who was living in one room which had no fireplace and in which he was obliged to sit up at night to keep the rats away while his wife and child slept. When I have repeated that experience to other people, they have been incredulous and said that "the sanitary inspector would not allow it." But I was speaking of things I had seen and knew to be true and unexaggerated. It is a terrible indictment of a Christian country that such circumstances should be permitted to make the way of the good life harder than it ever need be.

It was before the war also, and when housing conditions were quite uncomplicated by bombing, that a discussion took place on the B.B.C. on slum clearance. The then Minister of Health took part. One slum dweller made a corroborated statement that in the house where he lived there were six families in seven rooms— thirty-one people altogether. "It's damp," he said. "The plaster is damp, the floor boards are rotted so that we have to put tins over them. We can't leave the babies alone because of the rats. We all sleep in one room and hear the rats scratching continually." He paid fourteen shillings, six pence a week for this basement, and with gas it came to nineteen shillings.

It is not *impossible* to live a Christian life under such circumstances, but who will deny that it is desperately hard?

Recently I revisited the old walled town of Conway in North Wales where I began my ordained ministry. There is a famous suspension bridge there, and, when I lived there, all but pedestrians had to pay a toll to cross.

Now, I crossed that bridge four times every Sunday for three years, and I never paid. Not once! I crossed it on my bicycle, and I crossed it in a car, but I never paid. The tollkeeper took one glance at me and waved me on.

I remember the mystery it created for some people at the time. They wondered—mistakenly—if I had a season ticket. "How do you do it?" they said.

The simple answer was this. I knew that there was an old Welsh law which said, "We cannot *make* people go to church, but, if they want to go, we will see that no obstacle is put in their way." Therefore, anybody crossing the bridge to go to church on Sunday, ministerial or lay, could cross without payment. A layman might pause to explain. My collar franked me through.

I honor the wisdom of those old legislators. It is, perhaps, not altogether surprising that it should be in Wales! "We cannot *make* you go to church," they said in effect, "but, if you want to go, we will put no hindrance in the way. Not even a toll shall stop you."

It is a parable. They were concerned to gather out the stones. So must we be. We cannot compel people to goodness, but we can construct an unimpeded way.

II

Having gathered out the stones, how can we set up an ensign? What *Isaiah* meant by an "ensign" it is hard to say. Was it a banner or some religious symbol set on a pole and shining in the gaze of all the people? We do not know. The question which concerns us now is: *by what means can we make the road to Zion inviting?*

A church-neglecting man is seldom arrested by sermons. For one thing he does not hear them. He is gay, and he wants to be gayer, and the only way to arrest him is to make him suspect that he is not gay enough. Therefore, I believe that the second thing we have to do is to *make righteousness appealing*, to make the path of virtue attractive, and set goodness in a lovely light. Those to whom the joys of religion are all strange would take a lot of convincing by argument that the pleasures of the world are cloying and overheated and not to be compared for one rational moment with the raptures of inward religion. To anybody who has really known both, what comparison that isn't odious can possibly be made between a compound of cabarets and night clubs and drinking parties on the one hand, and the unadulterated bliss of Christian fellowship on the other?

> O the pure delight of a single hour
> That before Thy throne I spend,
> When I kneel in prayer, and with Thee, my God,
> I commune as friend with friend.

Yet, it remains true that millions of our fellow countrymen, with no interest in religion at all, believe that they have the secret of gaiety, and that religion and dullness are synonymous terms.

The only strategy to commend to a Christian living in an alien environment and feeling the human loneliness of life among people to whom religion is nothing but a stale joke, is the strategy of their Divine Master; to let their light *shine* before men. Nothing provokes the interest and the envy of the gay so much as a gaiety more exuberant, more lasting, and more natural than their own, a gaiety which can appear in "the morning after" as well as "the night before" and subsides from ebullience not into a depressed reaction, as is the way with worldly gaiety, but into the bliss of inward peace. Not by forcing our views on the unwilling and fencing them into a corner to enquire "if they are saved" will we breach their defenses, but by living so radiantly before them that they will confess *themselves* that we have something that has passed them by. And there is the door open, and we have nothing to do but to walk in.

I often speak a defensive word for the Puritans. I hope to do so many times again. I think that one of the things which is wrong with our country is that the Puritan contribution has been scorned of recent years. The iron that these men put into the blood of our nation is a necessary element in our corporate health.

But I admit quite plainly that they had one chief fault. Too many of them left joy out of religion. They made life grey—almost literally so. John Milton's grey cloak was symbolic! Not even his friends would have said that there was much joy in his life, and its absence was not altogether due to his blindness.

Macaulay's strictures on the Puritans are well remembered. He said that they objected to bearbaiting, not for the pain it gave the bear, but for the pleasure it gave the spectators.

Some of that influence survives still in the Church. There are still folk among us who frown on mirth, to whom the most wholesome joke is irreverent, who filter all pleasures in an anxious way, who regard a visit to any entertainment as a lapse from grace, and who never impress people on their first contact as being full of the joy of the Lord.

I say deliberately that their depression and joylessness is a hindrance to many; so far from raising an ensign on the road of righteousness they put another stone in the way. They make religion repulsive; the path of virtue, when they are seen on it, becomes unattractive and righteousness far from winsome. It is, moreover, not true to the genius of our faith.

Christianity, whenever it breaks as living water fresh from the rock, bubbles out ebulliently. The early Franciscans, the early Methodists, the early Salvationists—all were exuberantly happy. They illustrate those fine words of Coventry Patmore:

All realities sing and nothing else will.

So let us meet the world with joy!—a joy that can survive even our sufferings and sorrows. Jesus said, "If ye loved me, you would have rejoiced, because I go unto the Father."

Our tribulations need not cancel it out. In our tribulations he said that we were to "be of good cheer." Paul called our trials "light afflictions."

When I was a small boy I remember asking my father why in so many old London houses (our own among them) there are windows blocked up. (They are still not uncommon in our city.)

"Oh, that was the window tax," he told me.

I have looked it up since. It was one of the maddest taxes that has ever been imposed. It was imposed, I believe, first in 1695 and was still in force in 1851. Every house that had more than six windows was liable to tax for the extra ones and many people, to avoid the tax, had the windows blocked up. Think of it! The government put a tax on sunshine. They deliberately shut out the light.

There must be no parallel to that in the spiritual realm. We must let the light in. The earthly part of us must "glow with the fire divine." People seeing us should want to be like us. There should be something of awe, I suppose, in the recognition of holiness, but it isn't real if it does not woo.

156

You all know how dull, eerie, and mysterious a church can look at night, especially when it stands in a graveyard. Actually, it is full of rich color, but it is color which cannot be seen. Yet when the church is lit for worship, how beautiful it seems, not to the people within, but to the people without. It is always the people outside who get the glory of stained glass at night. The craftsman's art of other days glows on them as they pass by and is seen for the lovely thing that it is.

There is many a life strong in virtue and full of fine character but strangely repellant because the light of happiness does not burn within. It is the lack of *joy* which makes some good men and women unattractive. Joy is like the light in the church. It allows the passer-by to see the beauty that is there.

III

Let this word be added. When people feel drawn to the way of Christian discipleship, attracted by the "ensign" of joy in you, the sin and inertia in their soul will raise all kinds of objections to the new longings and seek to explain your radiant happines in other ways. They will say that you have plenty of money, no problems, and are physically fit.

There must be no cowardice or faltering or vagueness on our part when their self-confessed longing for what we have breaks from their lips.

We must point them to Christ!

Tell them in simple, homely, natural words what the hymn writer meant when he said:

> Christ of all my hopes the ground,
> Christ, the spring of all my joy.

Let them know that it was *religion* which did it for you. Overcome your shyness to tell them that the secret of it all is *Christ*.

A man, with no interest in religion and something of a martyr to self-pity, read an article in a paper one day so gay and confident that he tossed it down in sheer annoyance and said something bitter about the cheap optimism of people who had never suffered as he had done.

Somebody picked up the paper and recognized the author.

"You can't say *that* man hasn't suffered," he said. "I heard him once."

The story came out. While still a youngish man the author had been forced to retire from his profession by a disease (incurable to medical science) which robbed him of his power to walk. Six years later his devoted wife, on whom he so completely depended, died of cancer at thirty-nine. He was left with a very limited income to fend for himself and his two children. Neither his faith nor his courage flagged.

Bewildered, the whiner said, "But how can a man with all that to endure write in this way?"

"Well," said his companion, "he has religion. He *really* has it. I've heard him talk of Christ in a way which left me in no doubt that he knows him personally, quite friends in fact."

That is how to nail it home. Don't let people think your joy arises from easy circumstances, good health, and no troubles. If there is anything in you really to admire, it comes from Christ. Gently, but quite firmly, get them to recognize that.

Let them know that it was real *religion* that did this for you. Overcome your shyness to tell them that the explanation of it all is . . . Christ.

So you will work with your fellow Christians to Christianize the social order and construct an unimpeded way.

So you will set up an ensign in your own radiant life.

So you will make clear to all who heed you that the open secret of it *all* is Christ.

16

What to Do When You Stumble

Overtaken in a fault—Gal. 6:1, K.J.V.

PAUL IS GIVING PASTORAL ADVICE IN THIS PART OF HIS LETTER TO the Galatians. He is telling his readers how they should treat one of their own number who stumbles in the way. There is to be no spiritual pride and superiority, no contempt for the one who had fallen, no forgetfulness that temptation is the lot of us all. "Thrust your shoulder," he says in effect, "under the burden of that man's shame and so fulfill the law of Christ."

My friends, I don't believe you are failing in that ministry. I believe you are tender not only to the tempted but to those who yield to temptation. It is another—and related word—of which I have reason to believe you stand in need.

How do you deal with *yourself* when you have been overtaken in a fault? All of us stumble at times. Some of us crash. Others may, or may not, know about it, but we know and God knows! How do we handle ourselves in an hour like that? We may be tempted to wallow in the evil and deny that it is sin at all. We may make restitution and feel, falsely, that restitution (important and necessary as it is when possible) has canceled out the sin. We may be so engulfed in shame that we just give up.

Let me see, as one sinner talking to others, if I can help you at that very point.

I

First, *don't minimize the sin.* Don't let yourself off lightly. If, indeed, it was a moral mishap, don't say that it doesn't matter. Never say about sin, "It isn't important." That is a lie, and a lie with awful penalties for your own soul. The Bible says plainly, "The wages of sin is death." The first thing, therefore, is to recognize the sin as a sin; repent the wrong you have done; claim forgiveness from God, and hate the evil for the loathsome thing it is.

Now, there are three common ways in which our guilty souls seek to avoid the admission of guilt. Sometimes we tamper with the labels. Sometimes we plead that the circumstances were peculiar. Sometimes we argue that times have changed. All of them are efforts to deny or minimize the guilt, and they are all perilous, because the first thing we have to do is to recognize it quite clearly, admit it to ourselves, and confess before God the evil that we have done.

Let us glance at those three traps in turn.

1. *Don't tamper with the labels.* Don't call a serious thing by a light name and try to sneak it past your moral guard. We began that practice in childhood. We called a lie a "fib," but it was still a lie. We did it (some of us) in the army. We called stealing "scrounging," but it was still stealing. Some people are doing it on buses and trains today. They aim to avoid paying their fare. It is robbery, but they call it "being smart." It isn't smart; it is plain thieving. Some people live a loose sexual life and call it "love." It isn't love; it is lust.

Years ago I attended a joint meeting of doctors, psychiatrists, and ministers to discover ways in which we could work together. There was a great deal of talk at that meeting about "pre-marital and extra-marital sexual relationships." I knew, of course, what they were meaning by all that, but there was one old rural parson present who was confused by the terms and couldn't keep his feet in the conversation. Finally, he said, "Pre-marital and extra-marital sexual relationships? Do you mean fornication and adultery?" I can recall now the astonishment those plain and biblical words created in that assembly. We like to gloss things over with less challenging names, and that is one of the ways in which we grease the path to sin.

Now, that is the first trap to avoid if you would never minimize the sinfulness of sin; don't tamper with the labels. You don't make a deadly thing innocuous by employing a light name. Cancer is still cancer, even when you call it "a bit of indigestion."

2. Here is the second trap. *Don't deceive yourself into supposing that sin is ever justified by circumstances.*

How did you get into that guilty relationship, through loneliness—*just* through loneliness? "The Lord knoweth," says the Bible, "how to deliver the godly out of temptation."

Other people are lonely and don't get into that. The loneliness was only a factor. The lack of firm moral principle was the real cause, a failure to claim and use the help of God.

How did you come to pass on that slander? Somebody told you?

But people often tell untruths. Did you not scrutinize it? Did you not first inquire whether it had any foundation in fact?

No, you were *eager* to pass it on. Why? Because you did not like the person about whom that slander was made. Jealousy gave it currency. You *wanted* to believe it.

Oh, don't excuse yourself in these things on the ground of circumstances! Admit the sin. There is nothing so healthy, nothing so disposing to spiritual healing than to drop all evasions and admit the fault.

Two or three weeks ago I crossed Holland. It was all done in a fast train in a couple of hours. What a little country Holland is!

What a poor country too, in some ways! A waterlogged swamp, much of it below sea level. What circumstances!

And in that mold of ugly circumstances one of the great peoples of the world grew up and contributed to art, to navigation, and to exploration some of the world's greatest men.

If people wanted to make an excuse of circumstances, the Dutch had it, but they turned the circumstances into triumph.

3. Here is the third trap. *Don't persuade yourself that morality varies from age to age.*

Among the many stupid phrases which people use to excuse their moral faults is to say of the severer ethical code of an earlier day, "Oh, that's Victorian!"

Listen! We are not dealing with the Victorian, the Edwardian, or the Georgian. Nor, for that matter, with the new Elizabethan. In morality we are dealing with the eternal God. When God gave the Ten Commandments, he didn't give them just for a few Semitic tribes and for one era in the long history of our race. He gave them to the Israelites, but, through them, to all humanity and for all time. They were meant to be the basis of all morality.

> Engraved as in eternal brass,
>   Thy mighty promise shines;
> Nor can the powers of darkness rase
>   Those everlasting lines.

And not the promise only, the Ten Commandments also:

> Engraved as in eternal brass,
>   The Ten Commandments shine;
> Nor can the powers of darkness rase
>   One everlasting line.

Time makes no difference to the moral counsels of God. It is for the Negro and for the Eskimo, this side of the "iron curtain" and that, for kings and commoners, and for every era of time. Custom may change but not the decrees of God. What chances to be in vogue may alter, like the shape of women's hats, but not the fiat of the mighty God.

Be on your guard against these traps, and you are not likely to fail in the first of our injunctions.

Be aware of the danger of tampering with the labels.

Be aware of the danger of making an excuse of circumstances.

Be aware of the danger of pleading that custom can affect God's moral demands.

Then you will not minimize your fault. Then you will see sin for the loathsome thing it is, and you will cry from the heart, "Have mercy upon me, O God, according to thy lovingkindness: according to the multitude of thy tender mercies blot out my transgressions."

II

Having accepted the forgiveness of God, *don't brood over the past.*

There are many people in the family of God who do not doubt God's forgiveness, but they never seem able to forgive themselves. The memory of their sin lacerates them. It is hardly ever out of their minds. So far from being able, as some are, to forgive themselves lightly, they seem unable to forgive themselves at all. Just like some unhealed wound in the body, this unhealed wound in the spirit drains their strength, hinders their progress, pours pus into the blood stream, and keeps them in a state of spiritual invalidism.

Let me talk to that need, because I know that some of you are in it.

God has forgiven you; *forgive yourself.*

Who are you to have superior moral values to the almighty God?

Here are two things which will help you to forgive yourself.

1. Can't you see that your unwillingness to forgive yourself is a form of spiritual pride? What you are really saying, at some deep level of your mental and emotional life, is this: "How could *I* ever have done that?" (Note the stress on the "I," the *undue* stress). "Me? A spiritual giant like me? A person who has had all the advantages that I have had? How I hate myself."

Now, look! That self-hate is doing you no good. It is, indeed, at that stage, doing you harm. It wakens the self-destructive principle in your nature. It is like poison injected into your veins. Accept the forgiveness. You cannot undo the past. God has forgiven it, and, if God has forgiven you, who can justly accuse you?

That is the first thing: *forgive yourself.*

2. Here is the second. In some mysterious way, beyond our human fathoming, *God can use sin.* I know it is mysterious, for sin is God's one intolerance, but the God who is mighty in creation is mighty also in transformation.

I point you to the Cross again. The Cross was the foulest thing our race ever did; it was the most sublime thing God ever did. The Cross was our worst; it was God's best. The Cross was our nadir; it was (if we dare use such a word of the All Holy) God's zenith.

Think now! You say you cannot forgive yourself? If you will really take that sin to God—*really* take it to him and not hug it to yourself—he will make something of it, something of your sin. Not by encouraging you, I think, to talk much about it, but to use it to drive the engine of your will, to quicken all your compassion to sinners, to show God's tender heart to the fallen, when other professing Christians might give the false impression that God is hard and unforgiving.

Have you ever wondered how Paul could toil on at his work as he did, year in and year out, in labors abundant and stripes above measure? What drove him on? The memory, among other things, of his sin. The recollection of the persecutions, the imprisonments, and the stonings he had inflicted on others. You might even suspect at times (though this would be a false inference I think) that Paul had not forgiven himself! The poet puts these words on his lips as Paul thinks of the saints he had ill-used:

> Saints, did I say? with your remembered faces,
>   Dear men and women, whom I sought and slew!
> Ah when we mingle in the heavenly places
>   How will I weep to Stephen and to you!

III

Finally, I would say this: *Don't fail to claim a perfect cure.* What do I mean by that? I mean that sin isn't necessary. "Ah, but," you say, "everybody sins."

I still say that "sin isn't necessary." The Bible promises that God will, with temptation, "make a way to escape."

Our spiritual fathers had a simple technique for convincing people that sin isn't necessary. They would say to those who seemed to argue that we *must sin*, "Can you live without sin for a minute? Yes? Can you live without sin for five minutes, for an hour . . . ?" You see how their simple logic worked. They did not argue that anybody but our Lord had ever lived without sin, and they didn't consider enough the state of sinfulness apart from separate sins. They just insisted that sin in a redeemed man *isn't necessary.*

Put nothing beyond the grace of God. You have no right to say that God never has and never will keep a redeemed man or woman without sin. Sin (we have said) is God's one intolerance. All the resources of heaven are engaged against sin. It is the purpose of God that you be holy. Charles Wesley sang:

> He wills that I should holy be;
> That holiness I long to feel,
> That full divine comformity
> To all my Saviour's righteous will.

Charles Wesley sang also about the miracles of life, the things which never could be and, yet, which God would sometime bring to pass, and he said:

> The most impossible of all
> Is, that I e'er from sin should cease;
> Yet shall it be, I know it shall:
> Jesus, look to Thy faithfulness!
> If nothing is to hard for Thee,
> All things are possible to me.

Don't fail to claim a perfect cure. Don't live in the mental state of those whose subconscious thinking runs like this: "All people sin. I must too." Paul answered that false reasoning when he said, "Make not provision for the flesh, to fulfill the lusts thereof." If you feel that only in eternity could God do this wonderful thing and that perhaps all eternity's too short to transform a nature like yours, think more on the power of grace. Is anything too hard for the Almighty? Have faith for holiness, even though the more you have of it, the less you realize that it is growing within.

Some of the greatest saints had been some of the foulest sinners.

I was reading recently the life of a woman who had been for years anybody's "pick-up," and today she is raised to the altar, entitled "saint," and receives the veneration of vast multitudes.

The God who took the foul-mouthed Peter, the bloodstained Paul, the lustful Augustine, and a million lost and undone sinners and made them not just "highly respectable" but made them saints will not deny his grace to you. *Transforming grace!*

Claim a perfect cure. However impossible this will seem to you (and however difficult the balanced theological statement of this truth undoubtedly is!), you must ever hold before you your true goal.

You have been overtaken in a fault? A serious fault? A "sin" you would call it, rather than a fault?

It is a time for great care.

Don't minimize your sin; go to God and get forgiven.

Don't brood on the past.

Don't fail to claim a perfect cure.

17

Paul's "Magnificent Obsession"

This mystery . . . Christ in you, the hope of glory
—Col. 1:27

I HAVE REMARKED TO YOU BEFORE HOW IMPRESSED I HAVE OFTEN been with the recurrence in Paul's letters of the phrase "in Christ." I never finished the toilsome task, but I got far enough to be in no doubt that Dr. Deismann, the German scholar, was right when he said that this phrase and its equivalents ("in the Lord" "in Him") occurs in the Apostle's writings no less than 164 times.

Think of it! We have thirteen letters of Paul, some of which are very, very short. Philemon is little more than a page. And yet, in this little precious sheaf of letters, this myriad-minded man uses one phrase no less than 164 times. What a great deal it must have meant to him!

Some evangelical Christians talk as though the whole message of Paul was his legal explanation of the atonement. Indeed, there are scholars who call this explanation the "Pauline Gospel" and make no reference to the apostle's doctrine of the Divine Indwelling at all.

It is not a reverent occupation to put into opposition related parts of the apostle's teaching (and I must be very careful myself not to be guilty of that now), but no one can talk intelligently

168

of Paul's "gospel" and leave out his absorbed concern about being "in Christ." Indeed, if we could say it without profanity, this repeated phrase was his "magnificent obsession." He couldn't get away from it. Over and over again it comes out and led William Law (John Wesley's one-time teacher) into a statement which some of you will think exaggerated too. Said William Law, "This is the whole Gospel, the birth of the holy Jesus within us; His conquering life overcoming our inward death." William Law said also, "A Christ not in us is . . . a Christ not ours."

I want to stress again what Paul calls: "This mystery . . . Christ in you, the hope of glory."

He calls it "a mystery," "a secret," though it is an open secret, a secret to be disclosed to anyone who is truly eager to share it. Not all who profess and call themselves Christians are in this secret. They may hold firmly to the belief that Christ is for them, but they have no experience of Christ in them. They may be ready to assert with the rest of us that they have an advocate with the Father, Jesus Christ the righteous, but they do not know him as a power within them, subduing the deep selfishness of their nature and thinking, feeling, and willing in the heart of his consenting servant. And it is because this second experience is so important that William Law said, "A Christ not in us is . . . a Christ not ours."

It is as though two men were suffering from some scabrous skin disease and both professed a faith in penicillin. One received the penicillin into him and was completely cured—the skin sweet and firm again and no adverse reaction of any kind. The other went about asserting his unshaken faith in penicillin, but he never received it, and he walks about diseased still. That was what William Law meant when he said, "A Christ not in us is . . . a Christ not ours." All that talk about the value of the wonder medicine, true as it is, is meaningless to one who doesn't receive it; a cure not in us is a cure not ours.

And that, in a sense, was what Paul was saying; you must have Christ within. The apostle had always strained after the highest in morality. His Jewish blood and Pharisaic training had insisted on the primacy of the spiritual in his life. From earliest youth the main bent of his forceful nature had been to keep the holy law. Yet he suffered constant defeat. He found in his nature another principle at work. Try as he would, sooner or later he crashed again, and at the last he cries, "The good which I would, I do not; but the evil which I would not, that I do . . . O wretched man that I am, who shall deliver me out of the body of this death?"

Now, it was this glorious open secret, this thrice-blessed mystery of the indwelling Christ which had brought deliverance to Paul. "Who shall deliver me out of the body of this death? I thank God, through Jesus Christ, Our Lord."

He knew now the answer to his need. It was not in Judaism. It was not in the most rigid form of Judaism—Pharisaism. He had a high faith, but it wasn't high enough. All his straining was self-effort at its best. Here was the answer to every beaten sinner. "Christ in you, the hope of glory."

Now, I want to bring out this truth by three negative assertions. Let the positive appear by implication! By showing you that other interpretations are not enough, let me point you to the heart of the mystery and make it still more clear why Paul exulted in it and repeated himself over and over again.

I

And here is the first assertion: *near is not enough.*

It is not enough—let it be said reverently—it is not enough to have Christ *near* to us.

Oh, it is wonderful, of course, in contrast with not even believing in his existence at all or knowing him only as a name, but, for the highest spiritual life, it is not enough.

You see, we do most of our living inside us. Our thinking, feeling, and willing are all within. External events press upon us, but they have meaning only by our inward interpretation.

We discover that when we are dealing with the troubles of life. The important thing is not what happens *to* us but what happens *in* us. The same thing can happen *to* two different people and a precisely opposite thing happen *in* them. Do you remember the two mothers, each of whom lost a boy during the war?—that crushing, awful bereavement. One of them turned sour and bitter and made her husband's life a misery. The other sobbed it out on the Saviour's breast and is one of the most sweet and trustful Christians that we know. The same thing happened to them; a precisely *opposite* thing happened in them.

Human beings do their main living within. A person can live in ideal external circumstances and yet have a mind haunted by fear or an imagination like a drain. A person, on the other hand, can live (like a woman I visited last week) with an invalid husband and a life largely made up of drudgery, but a soul as quietly reverent as a cathedral and with the breath of God about her all the time.

If, therefore, we are to be helped in our battle against temptation and in our war with fear and worry, selfishness and greed, we must have help *within*. Not *there*, but *here!* Not *outside*, but *inside!*

Paul's discovery concerned that very thing. The gospel gave *that!* It was that which made Christianity good news to him and not just good advice. God in Christ was able and willing to come right into the heart of his consenting servants and live there, teaching them to *love* like God, to *think* with God, and to *will* one will with God.

Paul never succeeded in explaining it, nor has anybody else since. He frankly called it a "mystery." How one personality can invade another, and yet preserve that person's essential freedom, baffles all psychological explanation. We know the steps to it: dedication, concentration, adoration—and the marvelous alchemy begins slowly to work. Yet it remains in its essence a mystery at the end.

All one can say is that it happens! People become Christlike. We see it at its best in the saints. No wonder Paul got excited when he began to experience the truth of it, and that he kept saying over and over again, "Christ in you; you in Christ." Near is not enough. He must be *in* you. "A Christ not in us is . . . a Christ not ours."

That is my first negative assertion: near is not enough. Here is the clue you need to answer the conundrum: "Who is the greater Christian—a learned theologian who can't keep his temper, or a charwoman who can't repeat the Nicene Creed to save her life, but who lives like an angel?"

Near is not enough!

II

Here is the second: *then is not enough.*

There is some Christian preaching and teaching which concerns itself only with the future. It is all about the better land, "far, far away." That is why the Communists have caricatured our gospel and called it "pie in the sky." That is why they have satirized the pulpit as a place where a preacher offers you a crown in heaven at the very moment when you are needing half-a-crown now!

It would be frank on our part if we admitted that *some* Christian preaching—more of the past than of the present—has concerned itself exclusively with the future. They left the "now" out. There was always "a good time coming"—usually beyond death. Immediate personal help, either with social conditions or in the individual struggle against sin, was simply not there.

And that, of itself, would prove that their message was not the gospel. One of the essential notes of the Christian gospel is "here and now." It is an immediate offer. The old gospel hymns prove it. Do you remember their characteristic phrases? "Make no delay"; "Do not tarry"; "Now poor sinner"; "Now to be thine, yea, thine alone." Charles Wesley sang:

> Father, now accept of mine,
> Which now, through Christ, I offer Thee;
> Tell me now, in love divine,
> That Thou hast pardoned me.

Three "nows" in four lines!

Then is not enough. I must have *now. Now* I want help in the struggle against temptation. *Now* I want peace in a world at cold war. *Now* I want sanity in a world gone mad. Now! Now!

"You have it," says Paul, "Christ in you *now.*" John says the same thing: "He that hath the Son *hath* eternal life." Has it now! I *must* have that quality of life! If I really have it now, death cannot touch it—not the life of God in the soul of man. To have it is to have it abundantly now, and eternally too.

A man or woman in whom Christ dwells is happy now. They don't have to wait till heaven to be happy.

When I was last in America they were telling me about a lady, not rich or in easy circumstances, but one radiantly happy with her faith and very sure of heaven.

Somebody asked her how she would feel if she was refused entrance into heaven at the last.

She rejected the idea. She insisted that in Jesus Christ she would *not* be refused.

"But," persisted the questioner, "*suppose you were*. Suppose, when you got to the gate of heaven, they wouldn't let you in."

"In that case," she said, "I would walk round the walls shouting out that I had had a very wonderful time on the way."

You see her point? Her happiness was not all of the future. This exulting happiness was hers *now*.

The *Birmingham Post* reported the other day that a Cannock miner had been summoned at Walsall for the nonpayment of maintenance to his separated wife. And this is what he said in the dock. These are the exact words: "I do not drink, and it is very rarely that I smoke, so I might as well be in prison as anywhere else because I get no pleasure out of life."

It is laughable in a way, and yet it is tragic, too. He speaks for millions of people to whom, it seems, there is no happiness even to be thought of apart from a pint and a pipe.

But then some Christians, as we all know, are very doleful too, not just doleful when they are in deep trouble (and God knows any man might be then!) but as their normal nature. They never look as though they live at "the secret source of every precious thing."

These people get our religion a bad name.

I went through the lovely village of Sils-Maria in the Upper Engadine during my holidays, and I remembered as I passed through that Nietzsche, the German philosopher, who was the spiritual father of Nazism, lived there for seven years. Did you know that Nietzsche nearly became a Christian once? And, when the decision was in the balance, he went and lived among Christian people reputed to be very devout—just to see what Christians were like! The experiment failed, alas! He said, "These

Christians will have to look a lot more redeemed before I can believe in it."

Do you normally look redeemed? Do you give the impression that Christ is *in* you? Does the earthly part of you glow with the fire divine? To be convincing you must be and look redeemed *now.*

III

Here is the third negative assertion: *now is not enough.* Does that sound a contradiction?

Near is not enough.

Then is not enough.

Now is not enough.

One of the many errors of the Marxists lies here. They put all the stress upon this life. Indeed, the Marxist has no faith in any other. He says that the only life we shall ever have is here. He asserts, in effect, that "Man is what he eats." When your breath leaves your body, you've had it! Now is enough.

Now is *not* enough. My whole soul cries out that it is not enough. If this is the whole of life, it is a cruel joke. If all our loves and hopes and dreams end in the passionless calm of death, we have been tricked. We are, of all men, most miserable.

Charles Wesley inquires:

> O who can explain this struggle for life,
> This travail and pain, this trembling and strife?

The atheist cannot. The agnostic is no better. The Christian can.

I stood in the cemetery burying a wife and mother in early middle life. I looked at that desolate husband and those two dear weeping girls, and I remembered this tonic word: "Christ in you, the hope of glory."

"The hope of glory." What a phrase! But is it only a hope?

Yes, but a New Testament hope, which you remember is "a sure and certain hope." Sure and certain! A hope which has no shadow of doubt, no trace of dubiety.

Now is not enough. We must have "then" also. Both! Now and then. Time and eternity. Earth and heaven. What a gospel! Every need is met. He who lives in our heart now will vindicate his indwelling in glory.

Sometime ago an army officer (it was Colonel David Marcus) was killed in action. Before he was buried, the contents of his pockets were put together and sent to his widow.

She was greatly comforted by one thing that he was carrying when he died. No, it wasn't a letter addressed to her; it was a little bit of paper entitled "The Ship." I don't know where the Colonel got it. I only know how much it meant to her:

I am standing upon the sea-shore. A ship at my side spreads her white sails to the morning breeze and starts for the blue ocean. She is an object of beauty and strength, and I stand and watch her until at length she is only a ribbon of white cloud just where the sea and sky come to mingle with each other. Then someone at my side says, "There! She's gone!"

Gone where? Gone from my sight—that is all. She is just as large in mast and hull and spar as she was when she left my side, and just as able to bear her load of living freight—to the place of destination. Her diminished size is in me, not in her, and just at the moment when someone at my side says, "There! She's gone!" there are other voices ready to take up the glad shout, "There! She comes!" and *that* is dying.

Christ in you, the hope of glory.
In . . . now . . . then . . .
Hallelujah!